Follow us @sacred.scribe.publishing and @evokealchemy
Tag us in your images #SacredScribePublishing
www.sacredscribepublishing.com

Seasons of Tarot, Tarot Spread Journal
Published by Sacred Scribe Publishing LLC

Edited by Leah Shoman
Designs by Emma Howard
All artwork by Emma Howard

ISBN 979-8-9879866-7-7

Printed and bound in China.

Introduction

This Journal Belongs To

....

Welcome to your tarot spread journal.
This is an enchanting, explorative journey of personal evolution and empowerment created just for you.

Discover different ways to deepen your soul enquiries, with both basic and extended spreads for all tarot reading abilities.

The journal is laid out in seasons to help you naturally align with your energetic centres and the rhythm of the universe.

May you find yourself amongst these pages, and enjoy embracing all of the secrets you hold within.

Love Always,
Emma

Contents

Contents

Autumn

Winter

Using Your Journal

This is where you will find the description of the spread you are using.

Here will be the basic spread questions

1

2

3

Choose to do the short spread or the extended version

Here you will find the extended spread questions

4

5

6

Date: ....../....../......

An affirmation relating to the spread

i.e I choose to create a day filled with kindness

What deck called to me to be used today?

i.e The Rider Waite Tarot Deck

What is my own interpretation of each card?

An area to write your card meanings

i.e Strength - I will move forward today with conviction

Ace of wands - There is potential for great success

Below you will find prompts to follow

What does my higher self believe the message of the reading to be?

i.e I know that I do not take myself as seriously as I could and I should be more assertive

How does this reading inspire me to take action?

i.e I feel supported to make decisions of my own and follow through

Numerology and Astrology influences

i.e 8 and 1 represent leadership and taking charge

Reflective thoughts & feelings

i.e This spread told me what I knew but was in denial of.

Intuitive messages

i.e I felt drawn towards the colour purple I know this is to encourage me to trust my intuition

Next 12 Months

This year-ahead spread helps you identify areas of growth and encourages reflection throughout your with this book. Begin by selecting a significator, a card representing your overall theme and energy for the year.

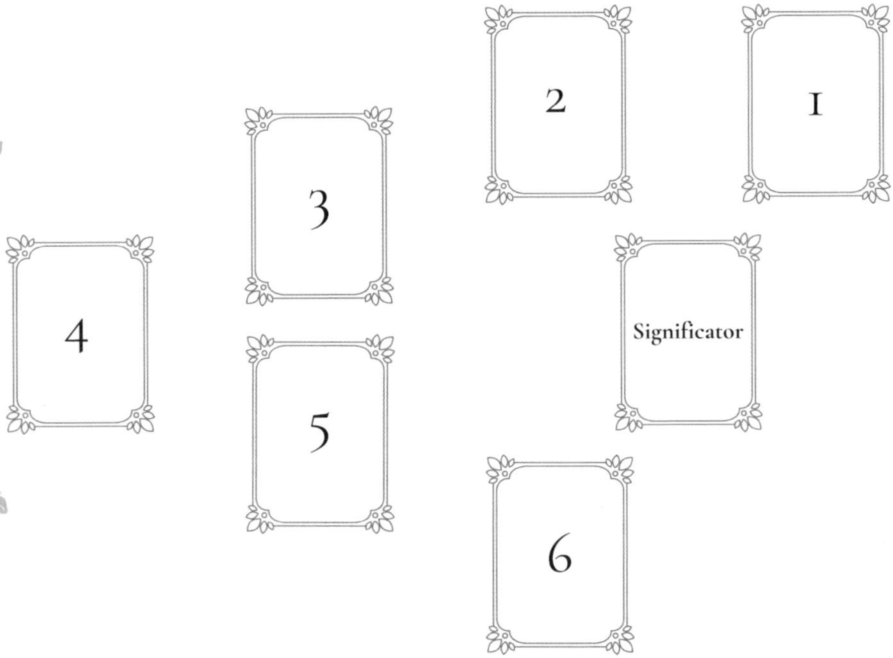

Spread questions

1 - January: What energy should I focus on to start the year?
2 - February: What is important in relationships this month?
3 - March: What opportunities are presenting themselves?
4 - April: What challenges will I navigate?
5 - May: What growth should I prioritise?
6 - June: What should I be more mindful of?

Next 12 Months

Lay out the cards in a counter-clockwise spread, finishing with the deck in the central position. Turn each card one at a time, noting your initial feelings. The card at the bottom of the deck is your shadow, highlighting an area to work on this year.

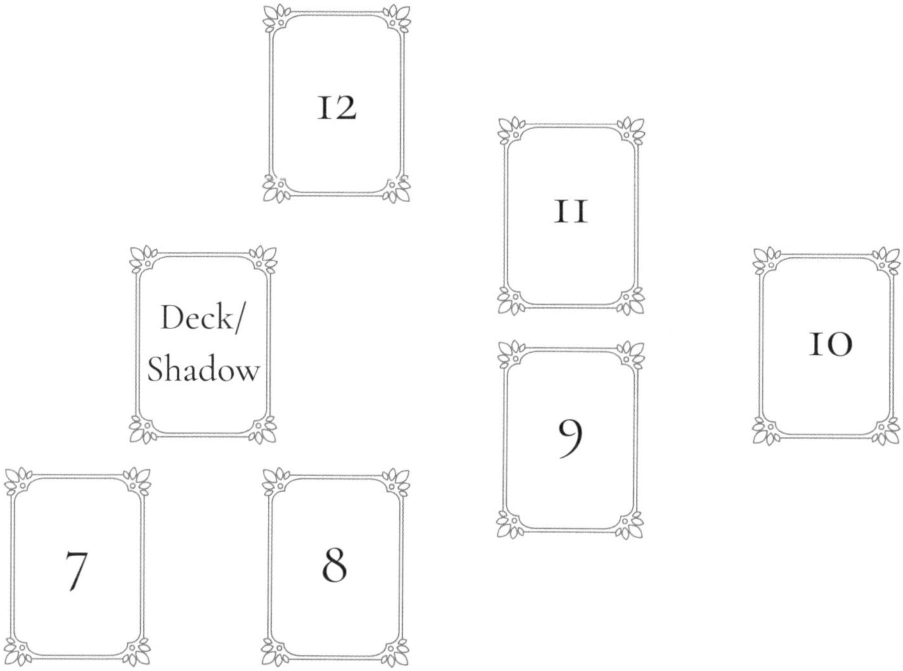

Spread questions

7 - July: What adventures await me this month?
8 - August: What lessons can I learn from the past?
9 - September: How can I focus my attention on my career?
10 - October: What spiritual insights do I need?
11 - November: What should I show gratitude for?
12 - December: How can I bring peaceful closure this month?

Date: ....../....../......

As I step into the new year, I embrace the infinite possibilities that lie ahead. I am open to growth, abundance, and joy.

Significator

....

January

....

February

....

March

....

April

....

May

....

June

....

Reflective thoughts & feelings

....
....
....
....
....
....
....
....
....
....

Intuitive messages

....
....
....
....
....
....
....
....
....
....

Date: ....../....../......

This year, I am ready to shine my light and live my truth.
I am empowered, I am deserving, I am ready.

July

....

August

....

September

....

October

....

November

....

December

....

Shadow/Bottom of the deck

....

Reflective thoughts & feelings	Intuitive messages
....	....
....	....
....	....
....	....
....	....
....	....
....	....
....	....
....	....
....	....

Spring

Spring is a season of waking up, unfurling, batting open the eyelids and feeling into our form again.

The spreads in this season are designed to gently ease yourself out from under the covers and feel supported and welcomed into the world.

Spring Tarot Challenge

Pick a card each morning for ten days. Reflect upon the meaning and journal your thoughts in the evening.

- Blooming Potential: What new opportunities are blossoming for me?
- Fresh Buds: How can I nurture my personal growth?
- Gentle Rain: What emotional cleansing do I need?
- Sunshine Days: How can I radiate positivity and joy?
- Spring Awakening: What should I focus my energy on?
- New Beginnings: What past patterns should I break?
- Growth Spurts: Where should I seek personal expansion?
- Nature's Renewal: How can I rejuvenate my spirit?
- Budding Relationships: What relationships will grow stronger?
- Spring Abundance: How can I attract abundance in my life?

Imbolc

Imbolc is celebrated on February 1st and marks the return of light. This spread represents the awakening of oneself and the cards are laid out in a pattern to symbolise growth.

Spread questions

1 - What shall I sow for my harvest to grow?

2 - What can I see that must change within me?

3 - What do I lack that I need to bring back?

Extended spread questions

4 - What should I leave and let go to seed?

5 - How can I light a fire to ignite my desire?

6 - What shall I cleanse ready to begin again?

Date: ....../....../......

Fire of heart, seed of womb I am ready to grow and bloom.

....

What deck called to me to be used today?

....

What is my own interpretation of each card?

....

....

....

....

....

....

....

....

....

What does my higher self believe the message of the reading to be?

....

....

How does this reading inspire me to take action?

....

....

Numerology and astrology influences

....

Reflective thoughts & feelings	Intuitive messages
....	....
....	....
....	....
....	....
....	....

Goddess Brigid

Brigid is the Goddess of Spring, fertility and light. This spreads marks the transformational phase of waking with the spring and is laid out in the shape of Brigid's cross.

Spread questions

1 - Ignite an intention for me to pursue?
2 - What focus for healing should I go to?
3 - Brigid give me a message to help me transform?
4 - From this new fire what will be reborn?
5 - A message from the well of inspiration.

Date: ....../....../......

I give myself permission to meet my needs today.

....

What deck called to me to be used today?

....

What is my own interpretation of each card?

....

....

....

....

....

....

....

....

....

What does my higher self believe the message of the reading to be?

....

....

How does this reading inspire me to take action?

....

....

Numerology and astrology influences

....

Reflective thoughts & feelings	Intuitive messages
....	....
....	....
....	....
....	....
....	....

Aligned

This spread represents the harmony between the chakras and our emotional and physical wellbeing. When we are aligned, we are in tune. The spread is laid to represent the upward current flow of energy over the etheric body.

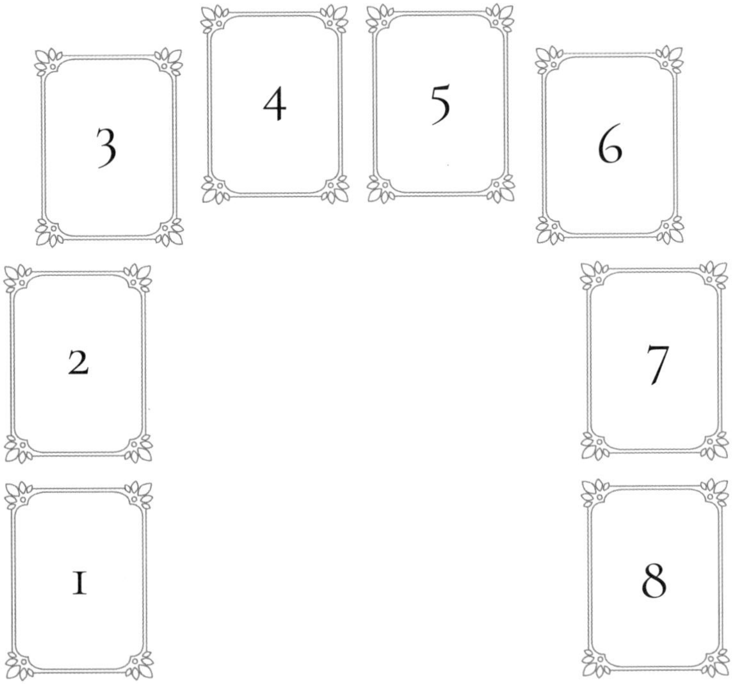

Spread questions

1 - Root chakra, what do I need to stay grounded?

2 - Sacral chakra, what should I fuel to ignite action within me?

3 - Solar plexus, what is my driving force at this time?

4 - Heart chakra, where can I soften towards myself?

Extended spread questions

5 - Throat chakra, show me my voice of authenticity?

6 - Third eye, how can I deepen my spiritual practise?

7 - Crown chakra, how can I learn to trust my inner wisdom?

8 - Soul star chakra, a message from my consciousness.

Date: ....../....../......

I am connected to my higher self and honour my needs.

....

What deck called to me to be used today?

....

What is my own interpretation of each card?

....

....

....

....

....

....

....

....

....

What does my higher self believe the message of the reading to be?

....

....

How does this reading inspire me to take action?

....

....

Numerology and astrology influences

....

Reflective thoughts & feelings	Intuitive messages
....	....
....	....
....	....
....	....
....	....

Spring Clean

This spread is designed with the intention of keeping our mind and home free of anything that can bring the ego into focus and take us away from our higher self. The cards are laid out in the shape of a horizon.

Spread questions

1 - What material things make my home feel cluttered?
2 - What habits are no longer supporting me?
3 - What thoughts and ideals have I outgrown?
4 - What emotional baggage needs to be released now?

Extended spread questions

5 - What can I eliminate from my schedule?
6 - How do I waste money that I could use in better ways?
7 - What will I do with all this space I've created for myself?
8 - What can be manifested now for my greater good?

Date: ....../....../......

Spring wash over me and breathe fresh air into my life.

....

What deck called to me to be used today?

....

What is my own interpretation of each card?

....

....

....

....

....

....

....

....

....

What does my higher self believe the message of the reading to be?

....

....

How does this reading inspire me to take action?

....

....

Numerology and astrology influences

....

Reflective thoughts & feelings

....

....

....

....

....

....

Intuitive messages

....

....

....

....

....

....

New Horizon

A spread for a time of change and uncertainty. Laid out in an arrowhead shape, a symbol of protection and strength.

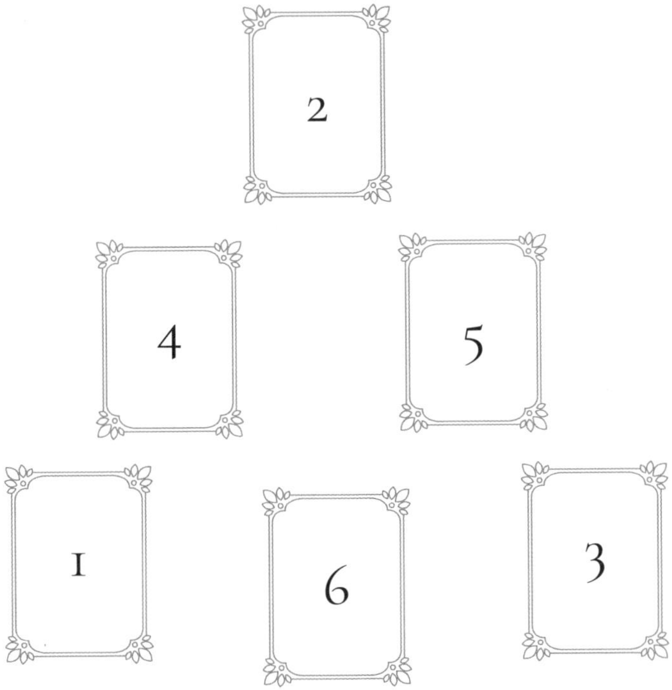

Spread questions

1 - I'm in a funk, point me in a new direction?

2 - How will this help me feel inspired?

3 - What has caused this separation in my heart and mind?

Extended spread

4 - What wonderful opportunities will this new direction bring me?

5 - Where shall I focus my energy first?

6 - Tell me something amazing about this new journey.

Date: ....../....../......

I embrace this new phase with open arms and an open heart.

What deck called to me to be used today?

What is my own interpretation of each card?

What does my higher self believe the message of the reading to be?

How does this reading inspire me to take action?

Numerology and astrology influences

Reflective thoughts & feelings

Intuitive messages

Eostre

Representing the spring dawn is the Goddess Eostre. This spread shows you the joys and blessings in your life and the abundance you bring to others. Laid in the pattern of a morning drop of dew, fresh and full of potential ready to water the earth.

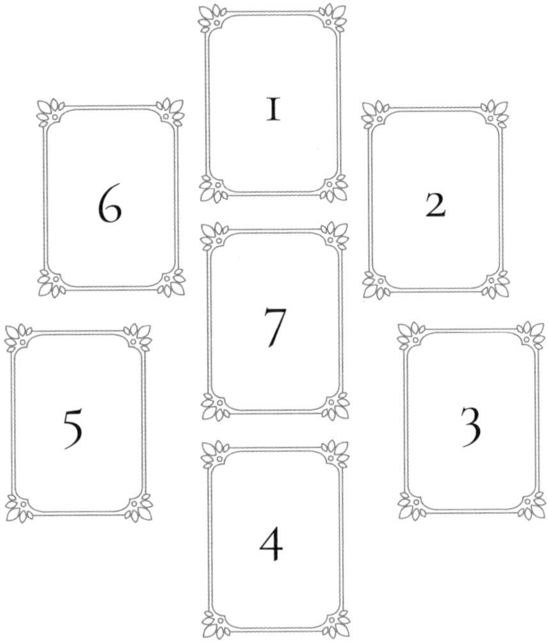

Spread questions

1 - Where do I bring the most joy to others?

2 - What blessings have I brought upon my own life?

3 - What light will tomorrow's dawn reveal to me?

Extended spread questions

4 - What ideas should I offer as gifts to another?

5 - What can I water within me to enhance my awakening?

6 - How can I celebrate myself this new day?

7 - What new blessings are coming my way?

Date: ....../....../......

All the gifts of a new dawn are within my reach I am pure potential.

....

What deck called to me to be used today?

....

What is my own interpretation of each card?

....

....

....

....

....

....

....

....

....

What does my higher self believe the message of the reading to be?

....

....

How does this reading inspire me to take action?

....

....

Numerology and astrology influences

....

Reflective thoughts & feelings	Intuitive messages
....	....
....	....
....	....
....	....
....	....

Windchimes

Attract positive vibes with this windchime spread. Laid out in a windchime pattern to bring in luck and prosperity.

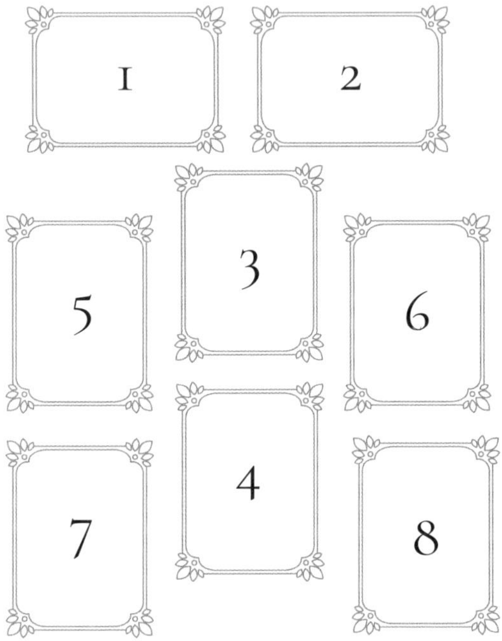

Spread questions

1 - What behaviour of mine prevents positive change?

2 - What obstacle can I blow away with ease first?

3 - How can I ring changes in my life today?

Extended spread questions

4 - What changes are coming my way that I am unaware of?

5 - How can I turn these changes into good luck charms for myself?

6- Where can I create luck this coming week?

7- What unexpected positive gifts am I to expect this month?

8 - Show me a quick change I can make to send luck my way?

Date: ....../....../......

I am safe and support myself becoming my best version of me.

....

What deck called to me to be used today?

....

What is my own interpretation of each card?

....

....

....

....

....

....

....

....

....

What does my higher self believe the message of the reading to be?

....

....

How does this reading inspire me to take action?

....

....

Numerology and astrology influences

....

Reflective thoughts & feelings

....

....

....

....

....

Intuitive messages

....

....

....

....

....

Freya

Freya known for photokinesis can light up her realm, but how can you bring light to your world today? This spread is laid out in the shape of the Freya rune.

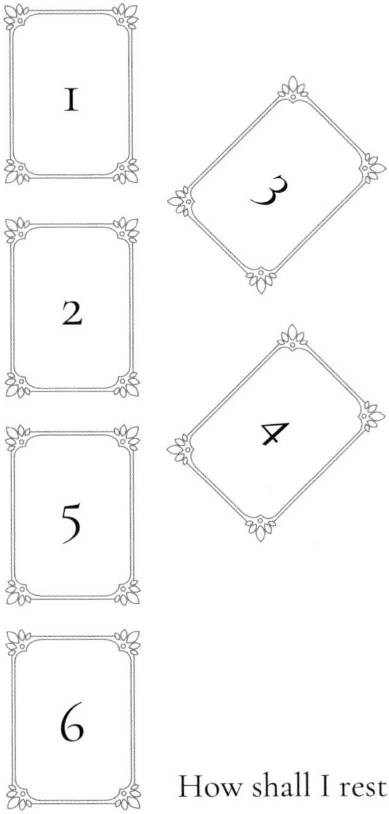

Spread questions

How shall I rest to recharge my light? - 1

Where will my passions begin to ignite? - 2

Where can I bring beauty to my life? - 3

Extended spread questions

What should I make a priority today? - 4

Where can I shine and empower my life? - 5

How will my inner light reassure those around me? - 6

Date: ....../....../......

I am a magnet for all that is good for me in my life.

....

What deck called to me to be used today?

....

What is my own interpretation of each card?

....

....

....

....

....

....

....

....

....

What does my higher self believe the message of the reading to be?

....

....

How does this reading inspire me to take action?

....

....

Numerology and astrology influences

....

Reflective thoughts & feelings	Intuitive messages
....	....
....	....
....	....
....	....
....	....

My Path

Where will your spiritual path lead you today?
Laid out in a winding little path moving forwards for spiritual enlightenment.

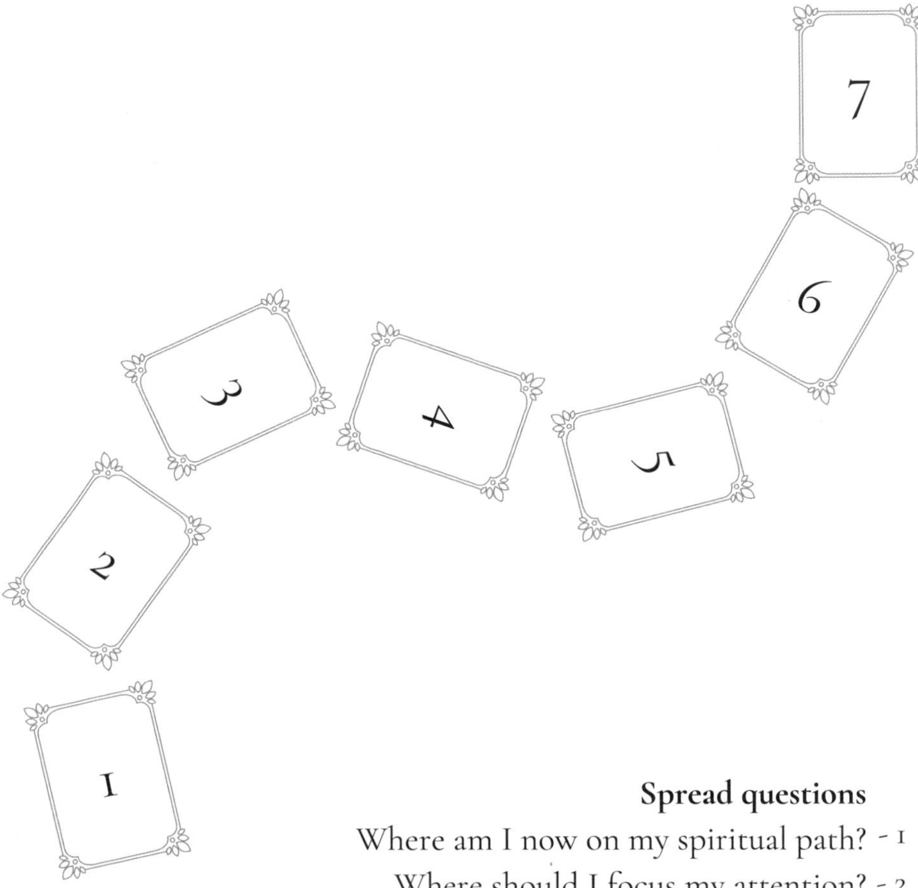

Spread questions

Where am I now on my spiritual path? - 1
Where should I focus my attention? - 2
What is of most importance for me to learn? - 3

Extended spread questions

What should I bypass on my spiritual path? - 4
How do I know this is right for me? - 5
Where can I learn from others? - 6
What is my greatest spiritual gift to share? - 7

Date: ....../....../......

My life is my own and I create my own path with love and joy.

....

What deck called to me to be used today?

....

What is my own interpretation of each card?

....

....

....

....

....

....

....

....

....

What does my higher self believe the message of the reading to be?

....

....

How does this reading inspire me to take action?

....

....

Numerology and astrology influences

....

Reflective thoughts & feelings

....

....

....

....

....

Intuitive messages

....

....

....

....

....

Dark Moon

The dark moon is a time to acknowledge what you want to push from your life. This spread is laid out in a moon for energetic flow.

Spread questions

1 - What should I bring to the surface?

2 - What should I look to clear and cleanse?

3 - Show me something currently hidden from me?

4 - Where am I deluding myself?

Extended spread questions

5 - What instincts cause me to not face my fears?

6 - What can I commit to giving my attention to?

7 - How can I be open to supporting my shadow through this transition?

Date: ....../....../......

I release all blocks and make space for new blessings to come.

....

What deck called to me to be used today?

....

What is my own interpretation of each card?

....

....

....

....

....

....

....

....

....

What does my higher self believe the message of the reading to be?

....

....

How does this reading inspire me to take action?

....

....

Numerology and astrology influences

....

Reflective thoughts & feelings	Intuitive messages
....	....
....	....
....	....
....	....
....	....

Lunar Eclipse

A lunar eclipse is a time for potential endings and beginnings. This spread is laid out as if an offering plate to the energies of the eclipse.

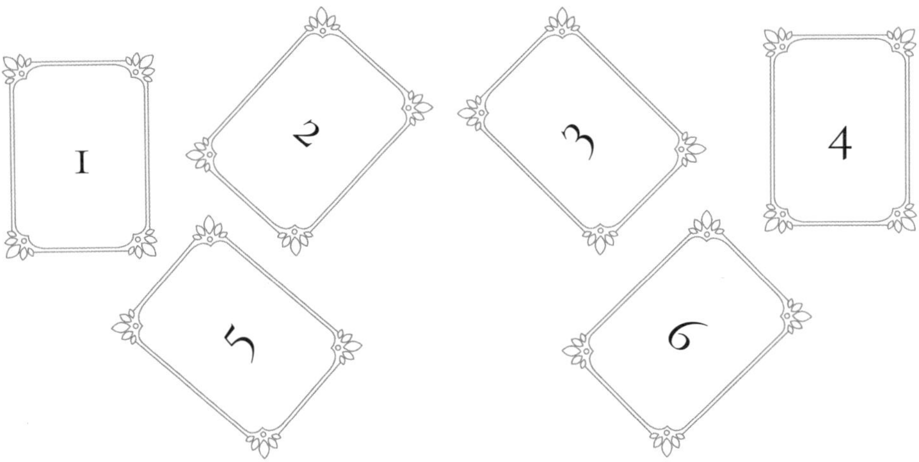

Spread questions

1 - Show me who I am right now?

2 - What card represents my life as it is now?

3 - Show me something to set in motion for the future?

4 - Where should I be reflecting on changing?

Extended spread questions

5 - A card to guide me towards new momentum?

6 - A card to show me what to focus my energies on?

Date: ....../....../......

I invite and enjoy a life of ease, truth, patience and peace.

....

What deck called to me to be used today?

....

What is my own interpretation of each card?

....

....

....

....

....

....

....

....

....

What does my higher self believe the message of the reading to be?

....

....

How does this reading inspire me to take action?

....

....

Numerology and astrology influences

....

Reflective thoughts & feelings	Intuitive messages
....	....
....	....
....	....
....	....
....	....

Blossoming

What potential is blossoming within you right now?
This spread is laid out in the shape of a flower blooming.

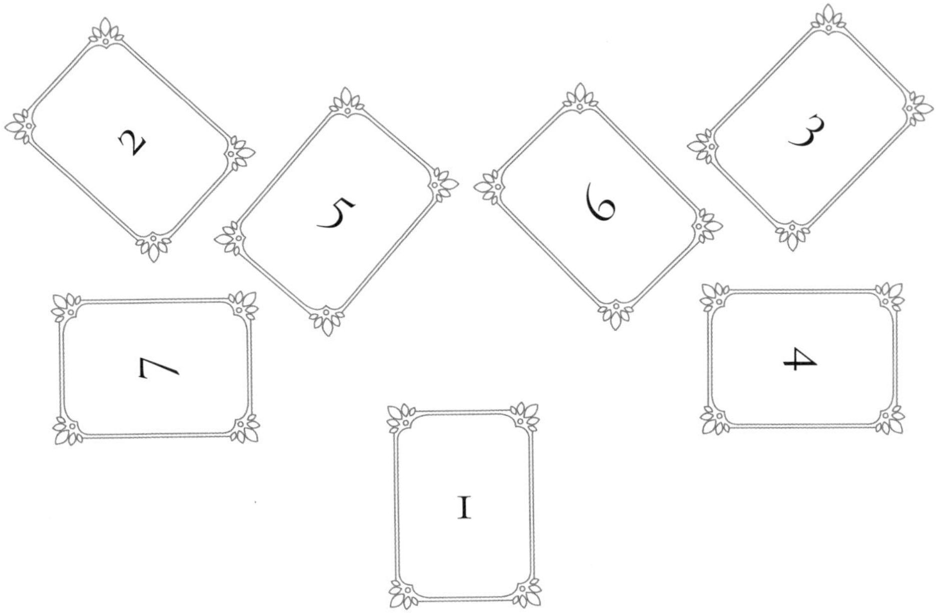

Spread questions

1 - What seeds of intention should I set at this time?

2 - What energies of light are supporting me?

3 - Show me what helps me to rise above and be open?

4 - What rain will shower blessings upon me?

Extended spread questions

5 - What can I do to bloom this season?

6 - Show me the storm that will test me?

7 - What rainbow will appear to brighten my days?

Date: ....../....../......

I bloom at my own rate and with everything I need to sustain me.

....

What deck called to me to be used today?

....

What is my own interpretation of each card?

....

....

....

....

....

....

....

....

....

What does my higher self believe the message of the reading to be?

....

....

How does this reading inspire me to take action?

....

....

Numerology and astrology influences

....

Reflective thoughts & feelings	Intuitive messages
....	....
....	....
....	....
....	....
....	....

Open The Window

Sometimes an open window is all we need to gain a fresh perspective. This spread is laid in the shape of a cloud, to allow your thoughts to drift upon.

Spread questions

1 - What aspects of my life need decluttering?

2 - What areas need clearing to make space for fresh ideas?

3 - What beliefs should I focus on sweeping away?

4 - What energies should I be welcoming in to me?

Extended spread questions

5 - What will I gain by inviting in new perspectives?

6 - What will I release that is keeping me stagnant?

Date: ....../....../......

I clear out old stale thoughts and invite in fresh inspiration everyday.

....

What deck called to me to be used today?

....

What is my own interpretation of each card?

....

....

....

....

....

....

....

....

....

What does my higher self believe the message of the reading to be?

....

....

How does this reading inspire me to take action?

....

....

Numerology and astrology influences

....

Reflective thoughts & feelings	Intuitive messages
....	....
....	....
....	....
....	....
....	....

My Garden

The garden is a place of retrospection, solitude, serenity and feeling supported by mother nature. This spread is laid out in the shape of a dragonfly, a symbol of understanding and realisation.

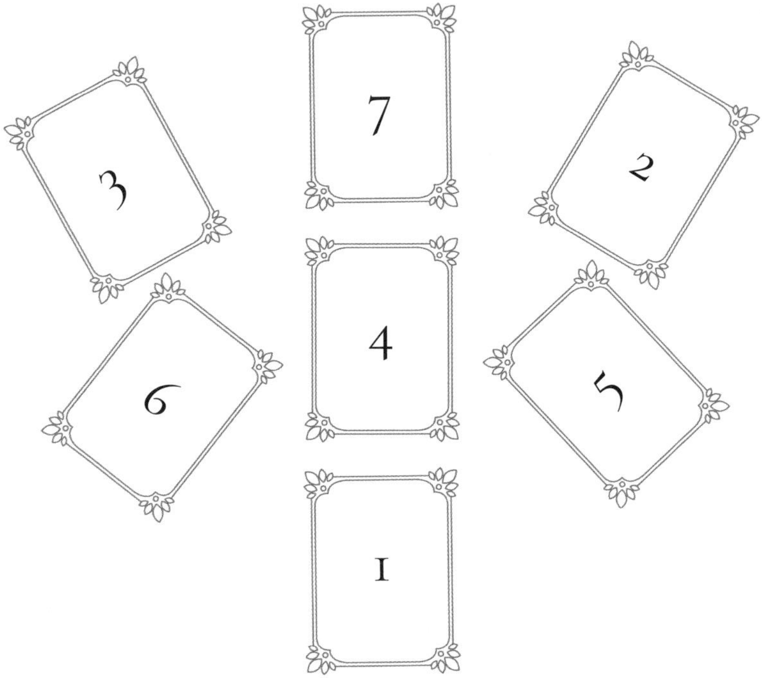

Spread questions

1 - Show me the soil that feeds my development?

2 - What card represents the things I am transforming?

3 - What vessel in my life am I placing my energy into the most?

4 - Where can I gain solitude and clarity with ease today?

Extended spread questions

5 - What weeds are stunting the growth I need to bring forth?

6 - How can I create space to nourish my soul for me?

Date: ....../....../......

I water the garden of my soul and encourage flowers to bloom there daily.

....

What deck called to me to be used today?

....

What is my own interpretation of each card?

....

....

....

....

....

....

....

....

....

What does my higher self believe the message of the reading to be?

....

....

How does this reading inspire me to take action?

....

....

Numerology and astrology influences

....

Reflective thoughts & feelings	Intuitive messages
....	....
....	....
....	....
....	....
....	....

Nature's Embrace

In nature, we ground our energy and connect with our souls deepest desires without fear. This spread is laid out in the shape of a well symbolising our sacred knowledge.

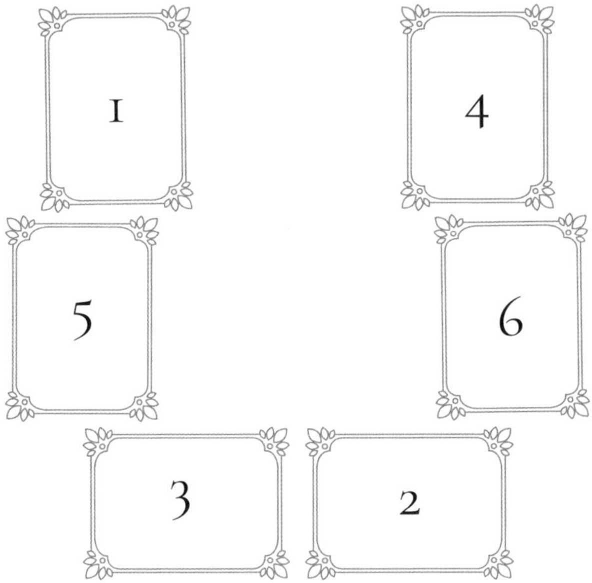

Spread questions

1 - Show me the grounding energy I need to embody?

2 - What mental clarity should I be seeking to gain?

3 - Show me the passion or motivation I need to move forward?

4 - What emotions should I be paying close attention to?

Extended spread questions

5 - A desire I deny and need to give love to?

6 - What spiritual lessons will reveal themselves to me?

Date: ....../....../......

I have knowledge that connects my roots to the earth and my spirit to the divine.

What deck called to me to be used today?

What is my own interpretation of each card?

What does my higher self believe the message of the reading to be?

How does this reading inspire me to take action?

Numerology and astrology influences

Reflective thoughts & feelings

Intuitive messages

Balance

Balance is a spread about weighing the positive and negative in order to find equilibrium. This spread is laid out in the shape of the scales of justice.

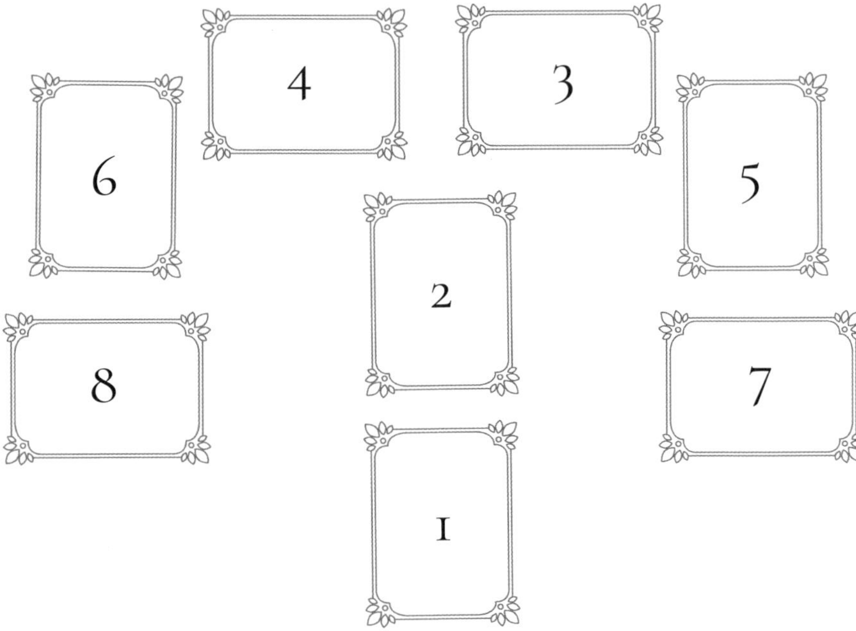

Spread questions

1 - Show me what illuminates my path for my highest good?

2 - What shadows or uncertainties do I need to address?

3 - How do I find equilibrium between opposing forces or situations in my life?

4 - What areas in my life are already in harmony?

Extended spread questions

5 - Where can I seek to find clarity in areas of doubt?

6 - What within me is ready to transform to allow more balance to emerge?

7 - Where should I give more energy?

8 - What will thrive when I find balance?

Date: ....../....../......

I make balanced, positive decisions for myself and my life daily.

....

What deck called to me to be used today?

....

What is my own interpretation of each card?

....

....

....

....

....

....

....

....

....

What does my higher self believe the message of the reading to be?

....

....

How does this reading inspire me to take action?

....

....

Numerology and astrology influences

....

Reflective thoughts & feelings	Intuitive messages
....	....
....	....
....	....
....	....
....	....

Create Your Own

Date: ....../....../......

Create your own affirmation relating to your spread.

....

What deck called to me to be used today?

....

What is my own interpretation of each card?

....

....

....

....

....

....

....

....

....

What does my higher self believe the message of the reading to be?

....

....

How does this reading inspire me to take action?

....

....

Numerology and astrology influences

....

Reflective thoughts & feelings

....

....

....

....

....

Intuitive messages

....

....

....

....

....

Summer

Summer is a season of growth, expansion, exploration and potential.

The spreads in this season are designed to challenge your perspective, recognise your worth and make plans to step out of your comfort zone.

Summer Tarot Challenge

Pick a card each morning for ten days. Reflect upon the meaning and journal your thoughts in the evening.

- Sunshine Card: Pull a card for what brings light into your life.
- Beach Vibes: Draw a card to see what to let go of.
- Growth and Blooms: Select a card for your personal summer growth.
- Heat of the Moment: Choose a card to reveal passions to pursue.
- Vacation Goals: Pull a card for your relaxation and focus.
- Picnic Basket: Look for a card indicating abundance and resources.
- Summer Adventure: Pick a card for a new journey or adventure.
- Bonfire Wisdom: Draw a card for wisdom from social interactions.
- Sunburn Alert: Pull a card for potential summer challenges.
- Evening Chill: Choose a card to unwind and relax at day's end.

New Role

A spread for when you're feeling a little lacklustre in work or day to day life. The spread is laid out in an upward spiral symbolic of advancement and personal evolution.

Spread questions

1 - I'm stuck in a rut, what can help shift my butt?

2 - My job/life is a drag show me what holds me back?

3 - What steps must I take for these cycles to break?

4 - Give me a sign how to make that dream mine?

5 - Am I on the right path, now there's no going back?

Date: ../../....

My mind is a friend to my body, I keep my thoughts positive.

....

What deck called to me to be used today?

....

What is my own interpretation of each card?

....

....

....

....

....

....

....

....

....

What does my higher self believe the message of the reading to be?

....

....

How does this reading inspire me to take action?

....

....

Numerology and Astrology influences

....

Reflective thoughts & feelings

....

....

....

....

....

....

Intuitive messages

....

....

....

....

....

....

I Expand

This spread is for opening up to the bigger picture and connecting with your mind, body and soul.

Split your deck into three piles as pictured. Pile 1 represents the mind, pile 2 represents the body, pile 3 represents the soul.

Draw one card from each pile for mind, body and soul per question.

Spread questions

1 - How do I hold on to old perceptions of self?

2 - How can I begin to release this energy?

3 - How will this expand my horizons?

Date: ....../....../......

I make space in my life for learning, growth and understanding.

....

What deck called to me to be used today?

....

What is my own interpretation of each card?

....

....

....

....

....

....

....

....

....

What does my higher self believe the message of the reading to be?

....

....

How does this reading inspire me to take action?

....

....

Numerology and astrology influences

....

Reflective thoughts & feelings

....

....

....

....

....

Intuitive messages

....

....

....

....

....

Motivation

This spread is for opening up to the bigger picture and connecting with your mind, body and soul. Laid out in an upward arrow, expressing the invitation for understanding, expansion and growth.

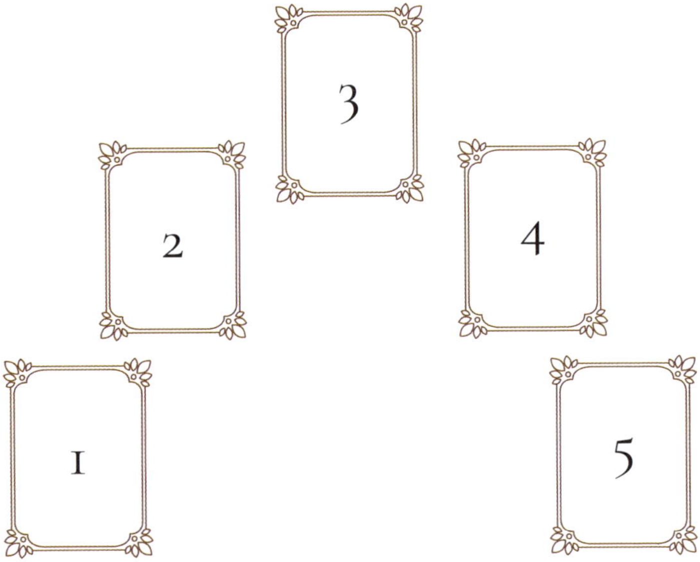

Spread questions

1 - Where am I striving to be right now?

2 - What has held me back thus far?

3 - How can I engage my hidden talents?

4 - Where can I create greater energy for success?

5 - Send me a message to get me started.

Date: ....../....../......

I make space in my life for learning, growth and understanding.

....

What deck called to me to be used today?

....

What is my own interpretation of each card?

....

....

....

....

....

....

....

....

....

What does my higher self believe the message of the reading to be?

....

....

How does this reading inspire me to take action?

....

....

Numerology and astrology influences

....

Reflective thoughts & feelings	Intuitive messages
....	....
....	....
....	....
....	....
....	....

A New Week

This spread is a light hearted way to invite and welcome new intentions and outcomes that you had not planned for. Taking steps towards a different outcome and perspective.

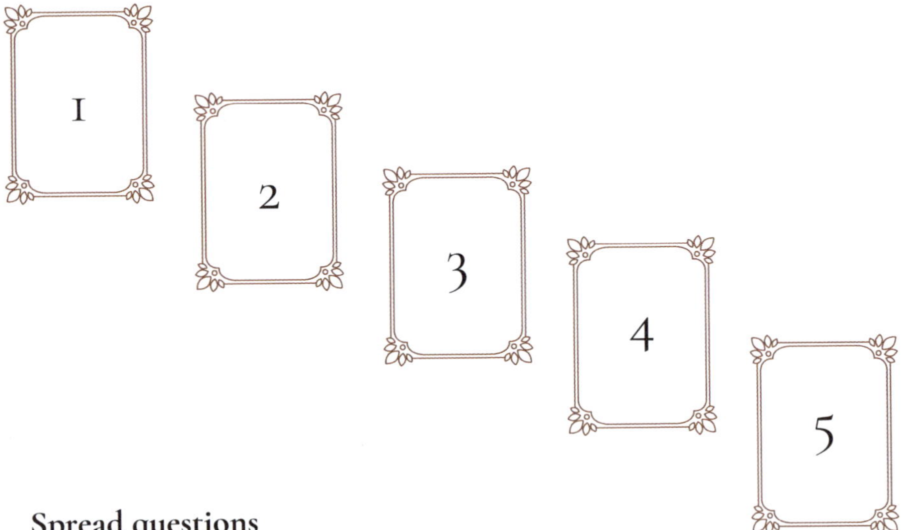

Spread questions

1 - How is this week looking?

2 - Any incoming surprise I should be aware of?

3 - What will help ground me this week?

4 - A reaction I need to be aware of?

5 - Where should I focus my energy?

6 - Where will I find my best self this week?

Extended - Please pull additional cards for clarification

Date: ....../....../......

This week is a magical gift and I pledge to enjoy every moment.

....

What deck called to me to be used today?

....

What is my own interpretation of each card?

....

....

....

....

....

....

....

....

....

What does my higher self believe the message of the reading to be?

....

....

How does this reading inspire me to take action?

....

....

Numerology and astrology influences

....

Reflective thoughts & feelings	Intuitive messages
....	....
....	....
....	....
....	....
....	....

Aim High

This spread looks at areas you can make small changes to encourage personal growth. It is laid out to represent forward momentum and a new trajectory.

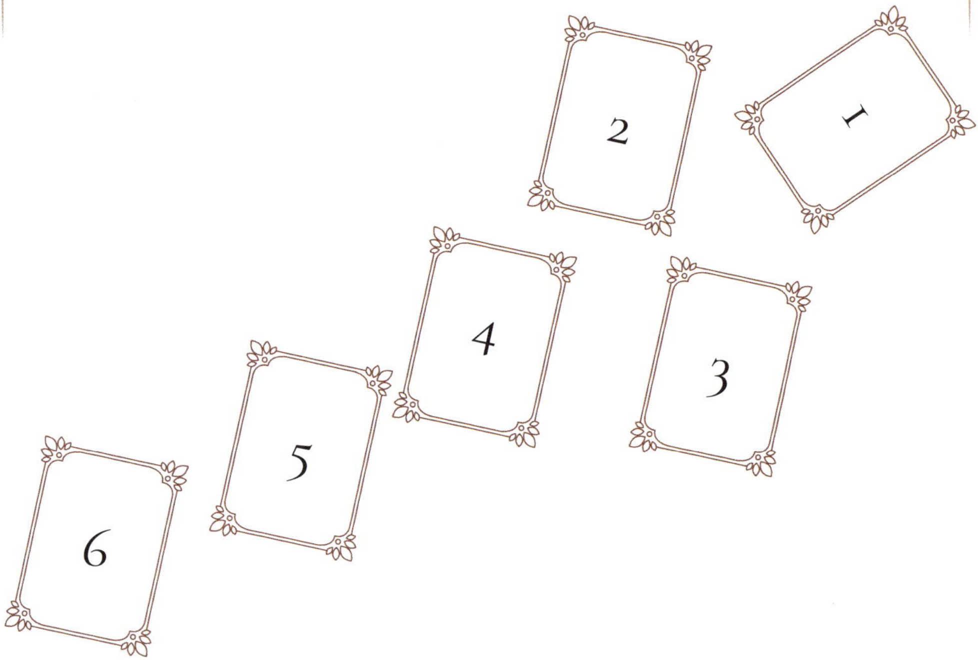

Spread questions

1 - My current position in life?

2 - What shadow shall I confront to help me ascend?

3 - Show me the target I should take aim for?

Extended spread

4 - What is my driving force?

5 - Where will my trajectory take me?

6 - Send me a message to help me soar.

Date: ....../....../......

I am effortlessly prosperous and highly successful.

....

What deck called to me to be used today?

....

What is my own interpretation of each card?

....

....

....

....

....

....

....

....

....

What does my higher self believe the message of the reading to be?

....

....

How does this reading inspire me to take action?

....

....

Numerology and astrology influences

....

Reflective thoughts & feelings	Intuitive messages
....	....
....	....
....	....
....	....
....	....

I Don't Know

This spread asks you to check with yourself and figure out how to know what you want. Laid out in a "Y" to represent the human form of the 'I don't know' gesture.

Spread questions

1 - I am confused, show me what causes my confusion?

2 - How can I tune into my inner no?

3 - Show me how to connect with my inner yes?

Extended spread

4 - What does my head want for me?

5 - Show me what my heart is seeking?

6 - What is it that I really need?

Date: ....../....../......

I am present and focused and take things one day at a time.

....

What deck called to me to be used today?

....

What is my own interpretation of each card?

....

....

....

....

....

....

....

....

....

What does my higher self believe the message of the reading to be?

....

....

How does this reading inspire me to take action?

....

....

Numerology and astrology influences

....

Reflective thoughts & feelings	**Intuitive messages**
....	....
....	....
....	....
....	....
....	....

Family Tree

This spread delves into your past, your family and your subconscious shadows to reveal layers that can be healed through recognition and understanding. It is laid symbolically as a family unit.

Spread questions

1 - What aspect of my childhood do I overlook?

2 - What aspect of my home life has been affected?

3 - How can I take a small step to reconcile that today?

Extended spread

4 - What element of the maternal archetype do I need to explore?

5 - What aspect of the paternal archetype should I heal?

6 - What childhood experiences caused me growth?

7 - Where in my upbringing did I lack nurture?

8 - How can my family support me better today?

Date: ....../....../......

I am capable of creating a family life I am very proud of.

....

What deck called to me to be used today?

....

What is my own interpretation of each card?

....

....

....

....

....

....

....

....

....

What does my higher self believe the message of the reading to be?

....

....

How does this reading inspire me to take action?

....

....

Numerology and astrology influences

....

Reflective thoughts & feelings	Intuitive messages
....	....
....	....
....	....
....	....
....	....

Old Habits

What old habits do you need to release? This spread is laid in an upturned horseshoe, recognising the need to allow things to flow when it is time.

Spread questions

1 - What within me would flourish if I didn't deny myself?

2 - What fear causes me to hide my real self from others?

3 - What habit should I spend time analysing today?

Extended spread

4 - Which belief system should I make steps to change now?

5 - How will this bring my golden shadow to the surface?

6 - What thought patterns deny me my dreams?

7 - What habit causes me to hide from myself?

Date: ....../....../......

I learn from my old habits and abandon all negative thoughts.

What deck called to me to be used today?

What is my own interpretation of each card?

What does my higher self believe the message of the reading to be?

How does this reading inspire me to take action?

Numerology and astrology influences

Reflective thoughts & feelings

Intuitive messages

Waxing Moon

The waxing moon phase is a period of hope, growth and intentions. Use this spread to help you focus your thoughts. It is laid out in a waxing crescent moon shape.

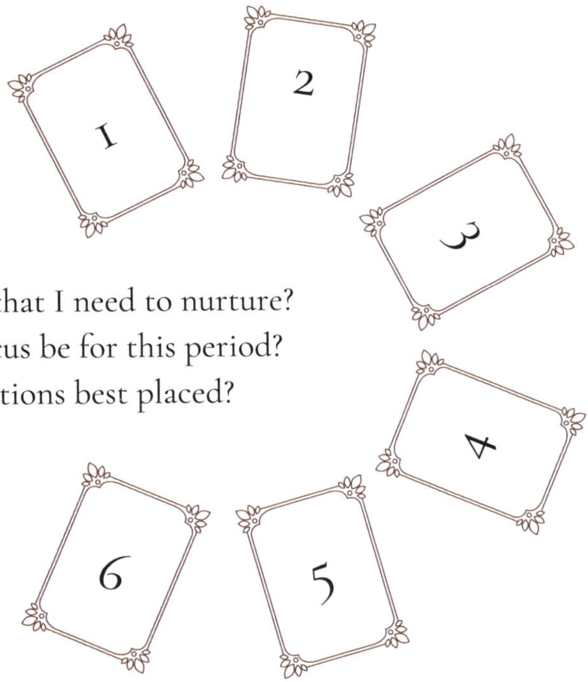

Spread questions

1 - What have I begun that I need to nurture?

2 - What should my focus be for this period?

3 - Where are my intentions best placed?

Extended spread

4 - What action should I take to help myself flourish?

5 - What opportunities will show up for me?

6 - What should I add to my life to encourage positive growth?

Date: ../../....

I am committed to my intentions and creating a life I want.

What deck called to me to be used today?

What is my own interpretation of each card?

What does my higher self believe the message of the reading to be?

How does this reading inspire me to take action?

Numerology and Astrology influences

Reflective thoughts & feelings

Intuitive messages

Solar Eclipse

The solar eclipse is a time to harmonise the masculine and feminine energies within us. This spread is laid out in a sun shape to honour her powerful energy.

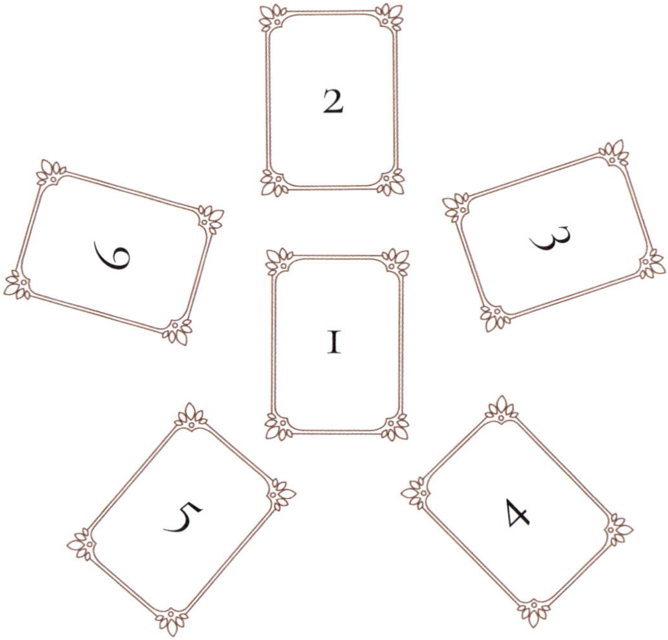

Spread questions

1 - What energy is waiting to erupt?

2 - What stagnant energy should I seek to remove?

3 - How can I harness the power of this solar eclipse?

Extended spread

4 - What will help me process that which needs to be removed?

5 - Show me the first step to create balance in my life?

6 - How can I harmonise the positive and negative aspects of my personality best?

Date: ....../....../......

I allow myself to receive as much as I give without question.

....

What deck called to me to be used today?

....

What is my own interpretation of each card?

....

....

....

....

....

....

....

....

....

What does my higher self believe the message of the reading to be?

....

....

How does this reading inspire me to take action?

....

....

Numerology and astrology influences

....

Reflective thoughts & feelings

....

....

....

....

....

Intuitive messages

....

....

....

....

....

I Am Shifting

Shifting is a state of connecting with a desired reality for yourself. This spread looks at the areas you need to grow and focus in order to shift. The spread is laid out in an upward arrow denoting ascendance.

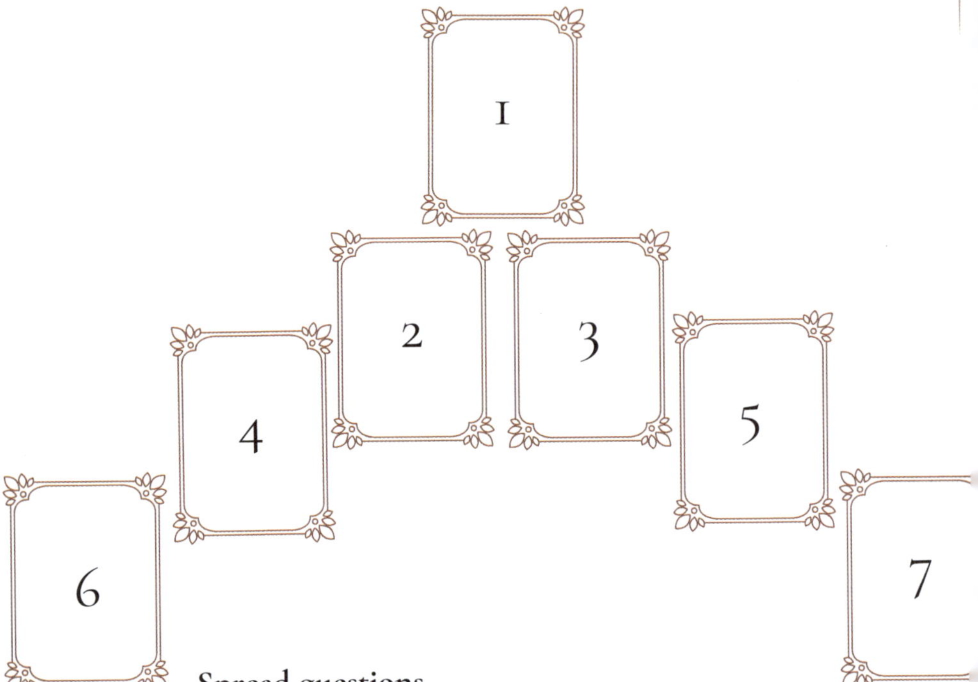

Spread questions

1 - Where am I on my shifting journey so far?

2 - What are my current blockages?

3 - Where do my strengths lie?

Extended spread

4 - What are my current blocks?

5 - Show me how to begin to address these?

6 - Where do I need to point my focus?

7 - Advice for the journey ahead.

Date: ....../....../......

My desired reality is in perfect alignment with my higher purpose.

....

What deck called to me to be used today?

....

What is my own interpretation of each card?

....

....

....

....

....

....

....

....

....

What does my higher self believe the message of the reading to be?

....

....

How does this reading inspire me to take action?

....

....

Numerology and astrology influences

....

Reflective thoughts & feelings	Intuitive messages
....	....
....	....
....	....
....	....
....	....

Illumination

This is a spread about noticing what lights you up, what makes you shine and how you can bring the spark into your daily life. This spread is laid in the shape of a fire, for comfort and warmth.

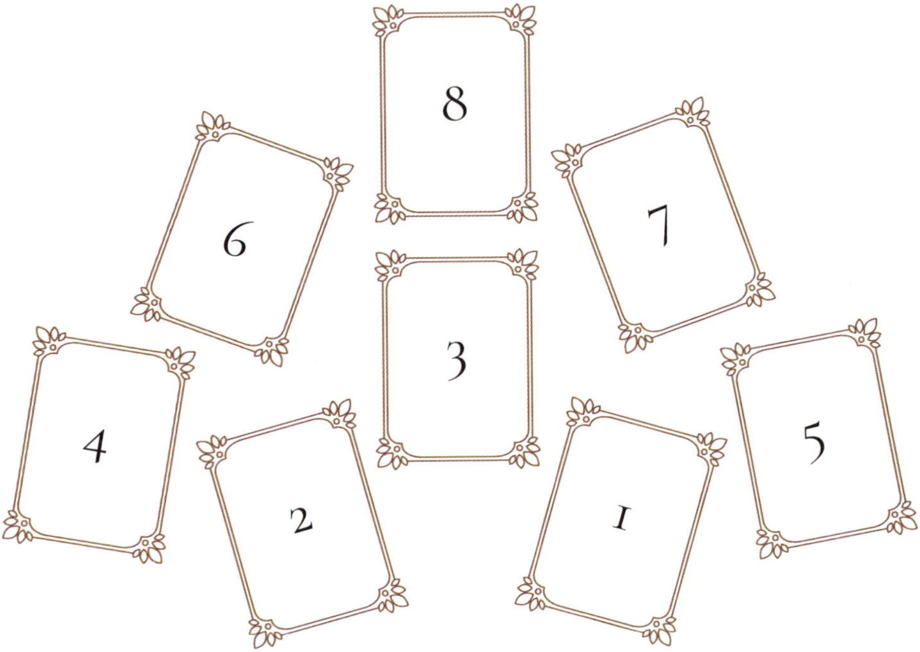

Spread questions

1 - What new beginnings will rise with the sun for me?

2 - What heat will I encounter during this time?

3 - What will come to closure when the sun sets?

4 - What dreams are written in the stars to come alive?

Extended spread

5 - What aspects of my core will I sustain?

6 - Where do I need to stoke the fire?

7 - Illuminate any hidden shadows?

8 - My eternal flame of desire is?

Date: ....../....../......

I am bright, fascinating and inspiring. I bring light to others lives.

....

What deck called to me to be used today?

....

What is my own interpretation of each card?

....

....

....

....

....

....

....

....

What does my higher self believe the message of the reading to be?

....

....

How does this reading inspire me to take action?

....

....

Numerology and astrology influences

....

Reflective thoughts & feelings	Intuitive messages
....	....
....	....
....	....
....	....
....	....

The Beach

The beach is a spread for reflecting on your current influences and surroundings. It is laid in a sandcastle shape to represent the constant building and evolution we experience.

Spread questions

1 - What energies am I basking in?

2 - What subconscious influences are rising with the waves?

3 - What dreams or goals am I successfully building on?

Extended spread

4 - What treasures of insight am I collecting?

5 - What boundaries keep me on the shore?

6 - Where should I seek shade and retreat?

7 - How can I hydrate my soul today?

Date: ....../....../......

I am a loving light being who leaves imprints on others souls wherever I go.

....

What deck called to me to be used today?

....

What is my own interpretation of each card?

....

....

....

....

....

....

....

....

....

What does my higher self believe the message of the reading to be?

....

....

How does this reading inspire me to take action?

....

....

Numerology and astrology influences

....

Reflective thoughts & feelings	Intuitive messages
....	....
....	....
....	....
....	....
....	....

My Harvest

This is spread for abundance and recognising what you have now and have grown from. Laid out in the shape of a cornucopia representing abundance and wealth.

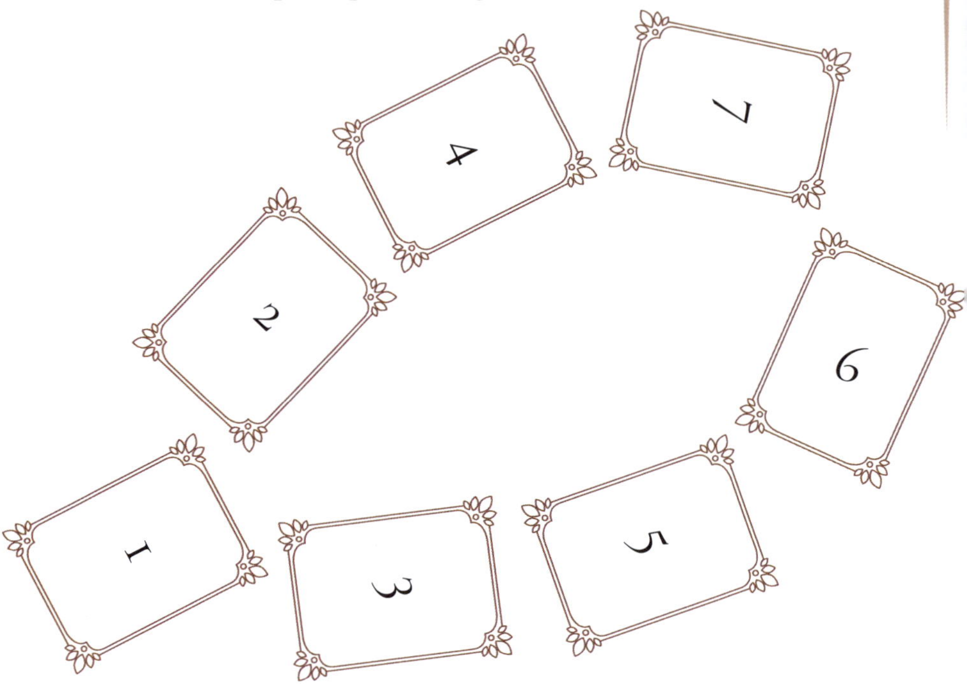

Spread questions

1 - What am I planting in my future?

2 - What is already flourishing?

3 - What manifestations are ready to be reaped?

Extended spread

4 - Where did I lose focus on my goals?

5 - How can I prevent this loss in future?

6 - Where am I most abundant?

7 - What blessings should I give thanks for?

Date: ....../....../......

I always receive what I need and I flourish with gratitude.

What deck called to me to be used today?

What is my own interpretation of each card?

What does my higher self believe the message of the reading to be?

How does this reading inspire me to take action?

Numerology and astrology influences

Reflective thoughts & feelings

Intuitive messages

Fire Within

This is an energy and empowerment spread, inviting you to find passion in your creative desires and is laid out in the shape of a heart.

Spread questions

1 - What ignites my desire right now?

2 - What do I need most to feel fuelled by my own fire?

3 - Where do I see new sparks of intention forming?

Extended spread

4 - What risks am I willing to take?

5 - Show me how to fan these flames of lust?

6 - Where can I challenge myself to grow?

7 - Advice for my transformation.

Date: ....../....../......

I am empowered to step into the fire and feel buoyed by the heat of desire.

What deck called to me to be used today?

What is my own interpretation of each card?

What does my higher self believe the message of the reading to be?

How does this reading inspire me to take action?

Numerology and astrology influences

Reflective thoughts & feelings

Intuitive messages

Adventures

This is a spread for exploration and redirection. Explore your challenges with a new perspective. This spread is laid in the shape of an arch or a path, the perspective is yours to choose.

Spread questions

1 - What is my current direction in life?

2 - What inner guidance is my compass at present?

3 - What resources do I have that are supporting my redirection?

Extended spread

4 - What challenges line my current path?

5 - How will they benefit my growth?

6 - What will my peak look like?

Date: ....../....../......

I grow from my changing landscape of life, as I weather the storms I am stronger.

....

What deck called to me to be used today?

....

What is my own interpretation of each card?

....

....

....

....

....

....

....

....

....

What does my higher self believe the message of the reading to be?

....

....

How does this reading inspire me to take action?

....

....

Numerology and astrology influences

....

Reflective thoughts & feelings	Intuitive messages
....	....
....	....
....	....
....	....
....	....

Create Your Own

Date: ....../....../......

Create your own affirmation relating to your spread.

....

What deck called to me to be used today?

....

What is my own interpretation of each card?

....

....

....

....

....

....

....

....

....

What does my higher self believe the message of the reading to be?

....

....

How does this reading inspire me to take action?

....

....

Numerology and astrology influences

....

Reflective thoughts & feelings	Intuitive messages
....	....
....	....
....	....
....	....
....	....

Mid Year Energy Check-in

This mid year energy check in spread looks at where we have come so far, and takes a peek into the energies coming forward in the next six months. Laid in the form of a person walking through an arch to symbolise transformation and the opening of new portals.

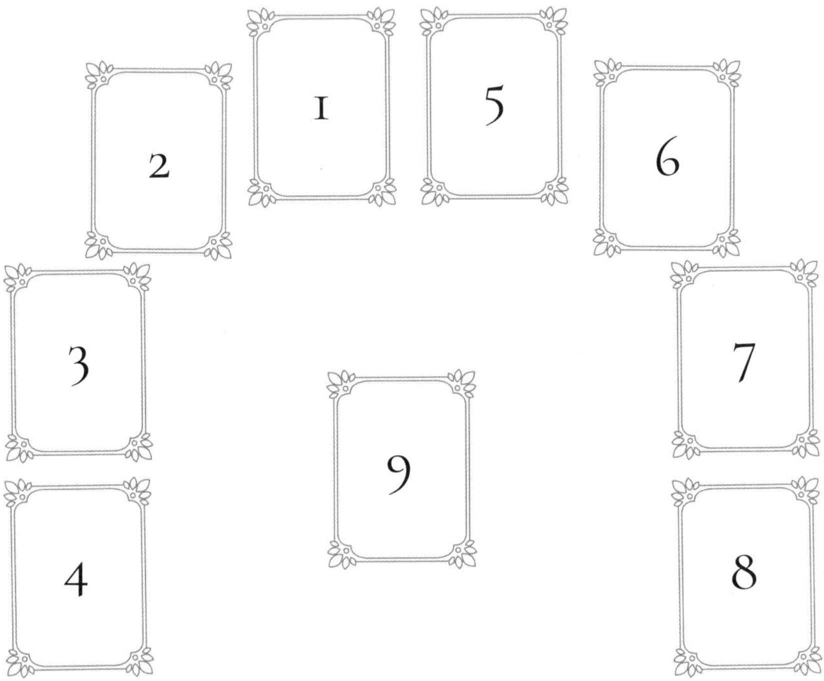

Spread questions

1 - What was the greatest lesson I learned in the last six months?
2 - What shadows have been healed?
3 - How has this helped rebalance me energetically?
4 - What will help to ground me in the next half year?
5 - What will be my main objective going into the next half year?
6 - How can I perpetuate this success and remain positive?
7 - Show me the shadow, person or situation I need to be aware of?
8 - What will be the biggest change coming in for me?
9 - A message from the Universe.

Date: ....../....../......

I affirm my strength and determination, I embrace energetic shifts for my growth.

What deck called to me to be used today?

What is my own interpretation of each card?

What does my higher self believe the message of the reading to be?

How does this reading inspire me to take action?

Numerology and astrology influences

Reflective thoughts & feelings

Intuitive messages

Autumn

Autumn is a season of success, achievements and reaping what we have sown.

The spreads in this season are designed to celebrate you, visualise new achievements, and softly ease you into your rest period.

Autumn Tarot Challenge

Pick a card each morning for ten days. Reflect upon the meaning and journal your thoughts in the evening.

- Falling Leaves: What should I let go of this autumn?
- Gathering Harvest: What strengths can I gather and use now?
- Cooling Breezes: How can I embrace change gracefully?
- Cozy Hearth: What will bring me inner warmth and comfort?
- Turning Colors: What are my current inspirations?
- Harvest Moon: How can I celebrate my accomplishments?
- Bare Branches: What hidden truths should I uncover now?
- Autumn Winds: How can I adapt to upcoming changes?
- Amber Glow: What brings me gratitude during this season?
- Twilight Hours: How can I prepare for the winter ahead?

My Superpower

When we know ourselves we can enhance our lives greatly. Lets reveal your special gifts with this spread. The cards are laid out in a wave symbolising taking action and making things happen.

Spread questions

1 - I know I have a superpower, show me what it is?

2 - What shadow dims my gifts light?

3 - How will I use this gift for world domination?

Extended spread questions

4 - How will I confront my shadow to use it for good?

5 - Show me the first step to activating my superpower.

6 - What card represents my superhero alter-ego?

Date: ....../....../......

Everything that is happening now supports my greatest endeavours.

....

What deck called to me to be used today?

....

What is my own interpretation of each card?

....

....

....

....

....

....

....

....

....

What does my higher self believe the message of the reading to be?

....

....

How does this reading inspire me to take action?

....

....

Numerology and astrology influences

....

Reflective thoughts & feelings	Intuitive messages
....	....
....	....
....	....
....	....
....	....

Goddess Selene

Goddess Selene rules the full moon and the moon controls the energies representing our emotional state. This spread will help you look into ways to use the energies of a full moon to your advantage.

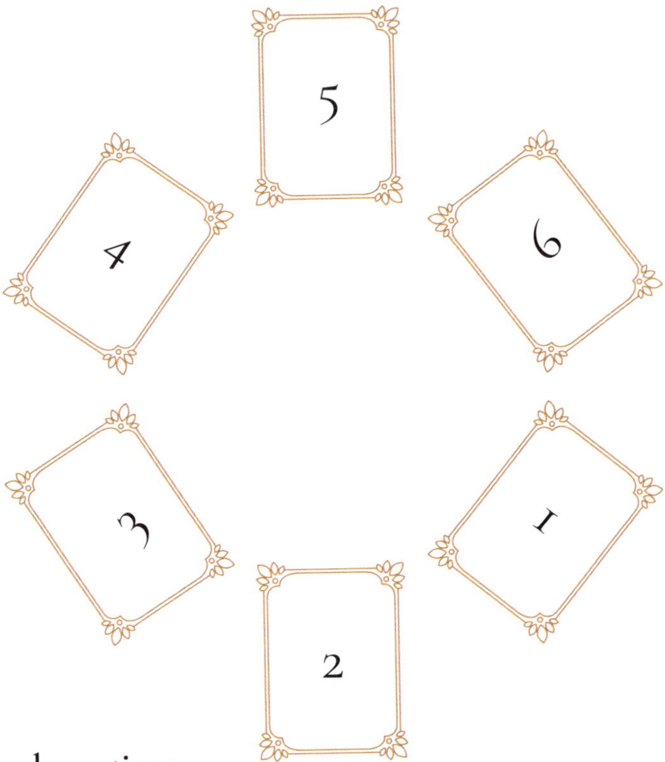

Spread questions

1 - Selene, what can you illuminate for me?

2 - How will you assist me to overcome this shadow?

3 - What feminine energy within me is ready to blossom?

Extended spread questions

4 - How will I transform during this lunar cycle?

5 - How can I use my inner light to support my sisters?

6 - Message of guiding light from Selene.

Date: ....../....../......

I am grateful for my resilience, strength and deep inner knowing.

....

What deck called to me to be used today?

....

What is my own interpretation of each card?

....

....

....

....

....

....

....

....

....

What does my higher self believe the message of the reading to be?

....

....

How does this reading inspire me to take action?

....

....

Numerology and astrology influences

....

Reflective thoughts & feelings	Intuitive messages
....	....
....	....
....	....
....	....
....	....

How's It Feel?

This spread questions how you or they feel about a situation. Laid out in a question mark to honour the quandary.

Spread questions

1 - What does this person bring to me emotionally?

2 - How does this person make me feel physically?

3 - Show me what I bring to this connection.

Extended spread questions

4 - What does my gut tell me about this situation?

5 - What does my heart tell me I need to pay attention to?

6 - A message from my higher self.

Date: ....../....../......

I trust my instincts without question, my gut knows what is right for me.

What deck called to me to be used today?

What is my own interpretation of each card?

What does my higher self believe the message of the reading to be?

How does this reading inspire me to take action?

Numerology and astrology influences

Reflective thoughts & feelings

Intuitive messages

Winning

This spread celebrates you and your goals and achievements. Laid out in a medal shape to honour your winning mentality.

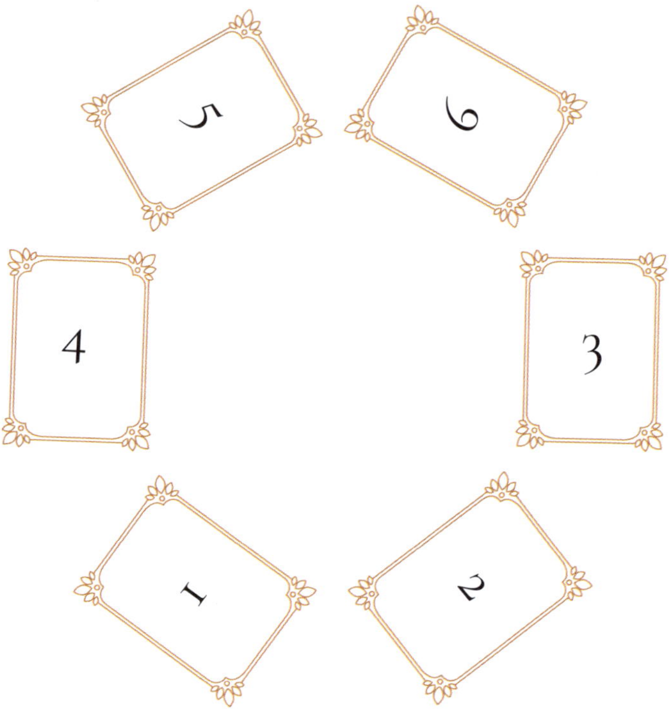

Spread questions

1 - What can't I see that's potential within me?

2 - What can I address to receive this success?

3 - Risks are fine, show me mine.

Extended spread questions

4 - Show me the reward that I will score?

5 - What do I have within that's going to help me win?

6 - What's my first task, that's my final ask?

Date: ....../....../......

I am successful in each of my endeavours, all are lessons in life.

....

What deck called to me to be used today?

....

What is my own interpretation of each card?

....

....

....

....

....

....

....

....

....

What does my higher self believe the message of the reading to be?

....

....

How does this reading inspire me to take action?

....

....

Numerology and astrology influences

....

Reflective thoughts & feelings

....

....

....

....

....

Intuitive messages

....

....

....

....

....

I Am Me

This spread has you recognise yourself and your abilities to create healthy boundaries to protect yourself. Laid out in the point of a bullet, showing taking control over your affairs.

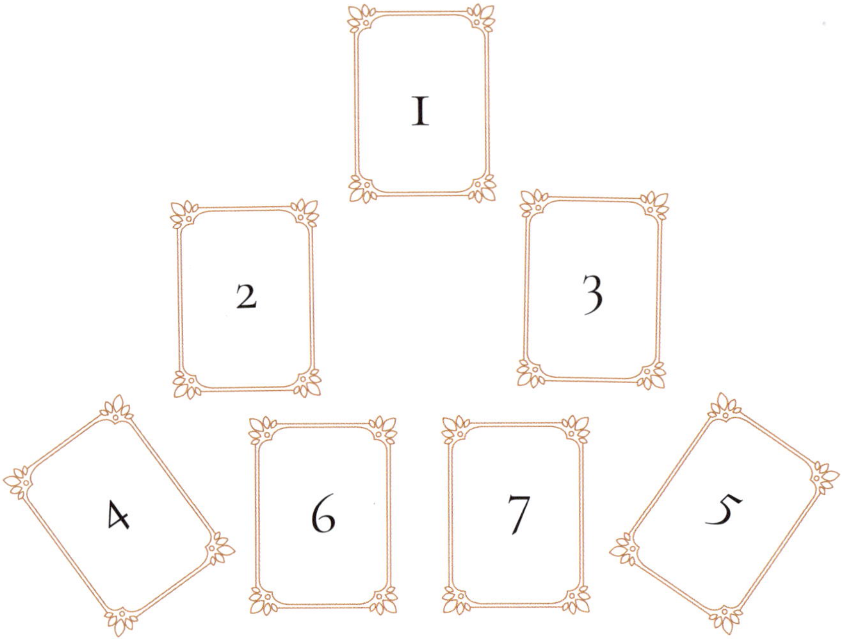

Spread questions

1 - What will help me detach from others negative energies?

2 - What shadow keeps me accepting this energy?

3 - Show me the first step to connecting with my inner yes.

Extended spread questions

4 - Show me the first step to connecting to my inner no.

5 - How is my own energy of value to others?

6 - Where can I regain my confidence to set healthy boundaries?

7 - Show me my initial step to get me on the right track?

Date: ....../....../......

I am confident in saying no to things that don't serve me.

What deck called to me to be used today?

What is my own interpretation of each card?

What does my higher self believe the message of the reading to be?

How does this reading inspire me to take action?

Numerology and astrology influences

Reflective thoughts & feelings

Intuitive messages

Plot Twist

This spread enables you to embrace change with an open mind. The layout is a double ended arrow, showing you torn in two directions or having multiple options.

Spread questions

1 - What plot twist should I be aware of ?

2 - What immediate effect will this have on me?

3 - What should I avoid that would affect me negatively?

4 - How can I harness the positive aspects of this plot twist?

Extended spread questions

5 - How will this impact those closest to me?

6 - What is the lesson I will see?

7 - What person will I become beyond this plot twist?

Date: ....../....../......

Plot twists accelerate my growth and open the gates wider to receive.

....

What deck called to me to be used today?

....

What is my own interpretation of each card?

....

....

....

....

....

....

....

....

....

What does my higher self believe the message of the reading to be?

....

....

How does this reading inspire me to take action?

....

....

Numerology and astrology influences

....

Reflective thoughts & feelings	Intuitive messages
....	....
....	....
....	....
....	....
....	....

Open Door

This spread questions life's circumstances they may have prevented you from taking great opportunities and walking through that open door. The spread is laid out in an open door inviting you to take a closer look.

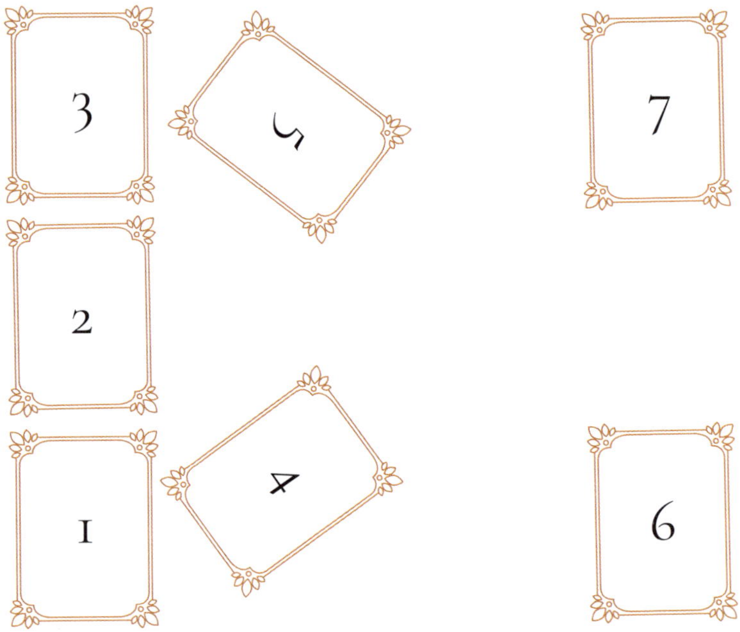

Spread questions

1 - Where am I most strongly influenced?

2 - What past experiences have attributed to this?

3 - How does my self image currently contribute to this?

4 - What from my past should I consider releasing?

Extended spread questions

5 - What am I averse to facing right now?

6 - Show me the shadow that holds me back.

7 - Where do I over analyse?

Date: ....../....../......

I recognise that new doors are always opening for me.

....

What deck called to me to be used today?

....

What is my own interpretation of each card?

....

....

....

....

....

....

....

....

....

What does my higher self believe the message of the reading to be?

....

....

How does this reading inspire me to take action?

....

....

Numerology and astrology influences

....

Reflective thoughts & feelings	Intuitive messages
....	....
....	....
....	....
....	....
....	....

Warm Embrace

This spread looks at how we embrace changes in our journey. Laid out like a flower to represent life's cycles and changes of destiny.

Spread questions

1 - What will the next phase of my journey look like?
2 - How will this change my current path?
3 - What action can I take initiate this new journey?
4 - What is most important about this change?

Extended spread questions

5 - What will hold me back from taking the initial step forward
6 - What must I understand first?
7 - What will evolve within me?
8 - How will I appear to others?
9 - A message from my higher self.

Date: ....../....../......

I am bold enough to embark on this new path with a warm embrace.

What deck called to me to be used today?

What is my own interpretation of each card?

What does my higher self believe the message of the reading to be?

How does this reading inspire me to take action?

Numerology and astrology influences

Reflective thoughts & feelings

Intuitive messages

My Vibration

This spread has a look at our energetic vibration for the law of attraction and is laid out in the symbol of vibrational energy.

Spread questions

1 - What is the energetic vibration I emit?

2 - What do I attract into my life currently?

3 - What residual energy pushes things away from my grasp?

4 - What will happen when I become more receptive?

Extended spread questions

5 - Where can I take the initial step towards raising my vibration?

6 - Who will this affect the most?

7 - How can I begin my manifesting process?

8 - What must I be more conscious of to effect this change?

9 - Advice to raise my vibration today.

Date: ....../....../......

I am a magnet attracting positive energy and emitting good vibrations.

....

What deck called to me to be used today?

....

What is my own interpretation of each card?

....

....

....

....

....

....

....

....

....

What does my higher self believe the message of the reading to be?

....

....

How does this reading inspire me to take action?

....

....

Numerology and astrology influences

....

Reflective thoughts & feelings

....

....

....

....

....

Intuitive messages

....

....

....

....

....

Shadow Self

Our shadow is the part of ourselves we don't portray to the outer world. We must honour our shadows in order to honour ourselves fully. The spread is laid out as open arms of the shadow welcoming the self.

Spread questions

1 - Unveil the darkest aspect of myself?

2 - Which area of my life is most affected?

3 - What is my inner demon?

4 - How do I begin to understand it?

Extended spread questions

5 - Where does this shadow hold me back?

6 - What can help me overcome this?

7 - Shadow give me a message of advice.

Date: ....../....../......

I welcome my shadow side into my light today with love and respect.

....

What deck called to me to be used today?

....

What is my own interpretation of each card?

....

....

....

....

....

....

....

....

....

What does my higher self believe the message of the reading to be?

....

....

How does this reading inspire me to take action?

....

....

Numerology and astrology influences

....

Reflective thoughts & feelings	Intuitive messages
....	....
....	....
....	....
....	....
....	....

Eclipse Rebirth

After an eclipse we begin a phase of rebirth, this spread will help navigate that transition. Laid out in the shape of the womb, symbolic for the rebirthing.

Spread questions

1 - How do I begin to unseat my ego self?

2 - How will my higher self guide me in this process?

3 - Where shall I start to evolve into my divine self?

Extended spread questions

4 - How can I replace my fear with self love?

5 - What will help me begin to trust this new process?

6 - Show me the gift that is born from this eclipse.

Date: ....../....../......

I encourage powerful and positive changes to be reborn.

What deck called to me to be used today?

What is my own interpretation of each card?

What does my higher self believe the message of the reading to be?

How does this reading inspire me to take action?

Numerology and astrology influences

Reflective thoughts & feelings

Intuitive messages

Autumn Equinox

The autumn equinox represents a period of change, an appreciation of both the light and the dark. This spread is laid out in the shape of the rising sun symbolising the light within and life force energy.

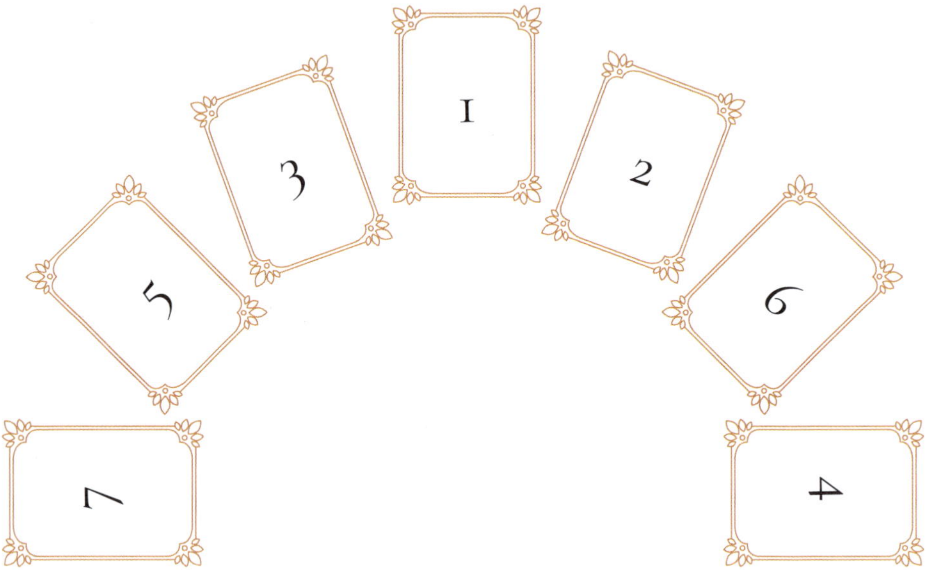

Spread questions

1 - What has risen within me since the year began?

2 - How have I healed as I've grown?

3 - What changes should I show most appreciation for?

Extended spread questions

4 - How can I prepare for this new darkening of the year?

5 - What will support this retreat and refocus?

6 - What will help harmonise these changes?

7 - What light will come from this new season?

Date: ....../....../......

I am ready to embrace the changing seasons and ease into my new skin.

What deck called to me to be used today?

What is my own interpretation of each card?

What does my higher self believe the message of the reading to be?

How does this reading inspire me to take action?

Numerology and astrology influences

Reflective thoughts & feelings

Intuitive messages

Falling Leaves

This spread represents the transformation and evolution we all face as we endure our life's cycle. The spread is laid top to bottom as a scattering of falling leaves would be. The symbolism that in order to continue to grow we must first lose something.

Spread questions

1 - What aspects of myself are naturally shedding?
2 - How will this cultivate growth?
3 - What opportunities will arise from this evolution?

Extended spread questions

4 - How can I stay grounded whilst experiencing this new era?
5 - What lessons should I be aware of?
6 - How can I integrate these into my current life?

Date: ....../....../......

I am awake to the changes that are happening and feel blessed and supported.

....

What deck called to me to be used today?

....

What is my own interpretation of each card?

....

....

....

....

....

....

....

....

....

What does my higher self believe the message of the reading to be?

....

....

How does this reading inspire me to take action?

....

....

Numerology and astrology influences

....

Reflective thoughts & feelings	Intuitive messages
....	....
....	....
....	....
....	....
....	....

Harvest Blessing

The harvest is a period of giving thanks for the gifts in your life and recognising the energy of love we emit and receive. This spread is laid in the shape of a pumpkin a symbol of harvest and abundance.

Spread questions

1 - What abundance is already mine?

2 - What lessons did I learn from this period of growth?

3 - Where could I receive greater support in my life?

Extended spread questions

4 - Who or what am I most thankful for?

5 - How should I share my blessings effectively?

6 - What will sustain me during the darker times?

7 - How can I remain grounded and focused for the changing times ahead?

Date: ....../....../......

I am grateful and share my blessings with generosity and love.

....

What deck called to me to be used today?

....

What is my own interpretation of each card?

....

....

....

....

....

....

....

....

....

What does my higher self believe the message of the reading to be?

....

....

How does this reading inspire me to take action?

....

....

Numerology and astrology influences

....

Reflective thoughts & feelings	Intuitive messages
....	....
....	....
....	....
....	....
....	....

Misty Morning

A spread to gain clarity or regain perspective. Laid in the shape of soft wisps of misty morning air symbolic of movement and the unknown.

Spread questions

1 - What fogs my perception at this time?

2 - What insights are waiting to reveal themselves to me?

3 - How will this bring me clarity and foresight?

Extended spread questions

4 - What am I being called on to reflect upon?

5 - What inner light guides me through these moments?

6 - What new clarity will bring me focus and drive?

Date: ....../....../......

I see everything as it is and I trust in the process of revelation.

....

What deck called to me to be used today?

....

What is my own interpretation of each card?

....

....

....

....

....

....

....

....

....

What does my higher self believe the message of the reading to be?

....

....

How does this reading inspire me to take action?

....

....

Numerology and astrology influences

....

Reflective thoughts & feelings

....

....

....

....

....

Intuitive messages

....

....

....

....

....

Ancestors

This spread guides us towards higher wisdom sent to us by our ancestors. It is laid out in the shape of the Ansuz rune, the symbol of ancestors, inspiration and communication.

Spread questions

1 - What wisdom or guidance do you offer at this time?

2 - What spiritual energies are surrounding me?

3 - What hidden aspects of myself are about to be unveiled?

4 - How can I honour the wisdom of the past into present day?

5 - What rebirth will occur as I connect to my ancestral roots?

Date: ....../....../......

I connect with my roots and honour my ancestral line with unwavering faith.

....

What deck called to me to be used today?

....

What is my own interpretation of each card?

....

....

....

....

....

....

....

....

....

What does my higher self believe the message of the reading to be?

....

....

How does this reading inspire me to take action?

....

....

Numerology and astrology influences

....

Reflective thoughts & feelings	Intuitive messages
....	....
....	....
....	....
....	....
....	....

Create Your Own

Date: ....../....../......

Create your own affirmation relating to your spread.

....

What deck called to me to be used today?

....

What is my own interpretation of each card?

....

....

....

....

....

....

....

....

....

What does my higher self believe the message of the reading to be?

....

....

How does this reading inspire me to take action?

....

....

Numerology and astrology influences

....

Reflective thoughts & feelings	Intuitive messages
....	....
....	....
....	....
....	....
....	....

Winter

Winter is a season of harmonising, reflecting, rest and resourcefulness.

The spreads in this season are designed to bring you to a place of quiet, draw inspiration from the past seasons and welcome in a period of rest.

Winter Tarot Challenge

Pick a card each morning for ten days. Reflect upon the meaning and journal your thoughts in the evening.

- Cosy Glow: Pull a card for what brings warmth into your life.
- Frosty Release: Draw a card to see what to let go of.
- Winter Growth: Select a card for your personal winter development.
- Fireside Passions: Choose a card to reveal passions to pursue.
- Winter Respite: Pull a card for your relaxation and rejuvenation focus.
- Snowy Abundance: Look for a card indicating abundance and resources.
- Winter Journey: Pick a card for a new journey or adventure.
- Winter Wisdom: Draw a card for wisdom from social interactions.
- Chill Alert: Pull a card for potential winter challenges.
- Nighttime Calm: Choose a card to unwind and relax at day's end.

Reflection

This spread determines where we project ourselves onto others. The layout is in the shape of a mirror or a pool of water, whichever you visualise.

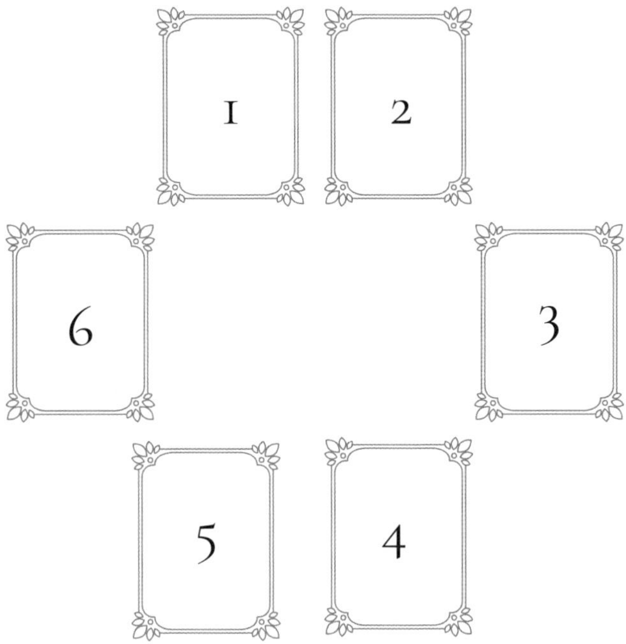

Spread questions

1 - How do I see myself?
2 - What do I unknowingly project onto others?
3 - What shadow can I tap into to create balance?
4 - How can I become more focused and less reactive?
5 - What is important to me right now?
6 - What is my real truth?

Date: ....../....../......

I embrace my past and honour my present learnings.

What deck called to me to be used today?

What is my own interpretation of each card?

What does my higher self believe the message of the reading to be?

How does this reading inspire me to take action?

Numerology and astrology influences

Reflective thoughts & feelings

Intuitive messages

And Rest

This spread will soften and ease you into rest. The layout is that of a deep warm cosy bed, waiting for you to snuggle into.

Spread questions

1 - How can I radiate warmth toward myself?

2 - What dims the light within at this time?

3 - How can I ignite my inner flame?

Extended spread

4 - How can I allow myself space to relax?

5 - How can I support others to nurture their inner flame?

6 - Where should I focus my compassion this week?

Date: ....../....../......

I ease into the flow of allowing myself times of peace and warmth.

....

What deck called to me to be used today?

....

What is my own interpretation of each card?

....

....

....

....

....

....

....

....

....

What does my higher self believe the message of the reading to be?

....

....

How does this reading inspire me to take action?

....

....

Numerology and astrology influences

....

Reflective thoughts & feelings	Intuitive messages
....	....
....	....
....	....
....	....
....	....

Soft Flow

This spread asks you to look at areas which stop your beautiful soft flow. The spread is laid out in a gentle wave to promote soft and steady flow.

Spread questions

1 - How can I be gentle and ease myself into this day?

2 - How can I navigate exhaustion?

3 - What will inspire me to take things more slowly?

4 - Who can I look to for help with this gentle flow of pace?

Extended spread

5 - What wave of emotion troubles me and puts me on edge?

6 - How should I soften my approach to this situation?

7 - Show me where to create a routine to focus on?

8 - What new flush of energy will come from this?

Date: ....../....../......

I honour the rhythms of my heart and encourage easy gentle flow.

What deck called to me to be used today?

What is my own interpretation of each card?

What does my higher self believe the message of the reading to be?

How does this reading inspire me to take action?

Numerology and astrology influences

Reflective thoughts & feelings

Intuitive messages

Winter's Darkening

A cosy spread to guide you into the darker evenings. Light a candle, get a warm drink and settle in for some soul enquiry.

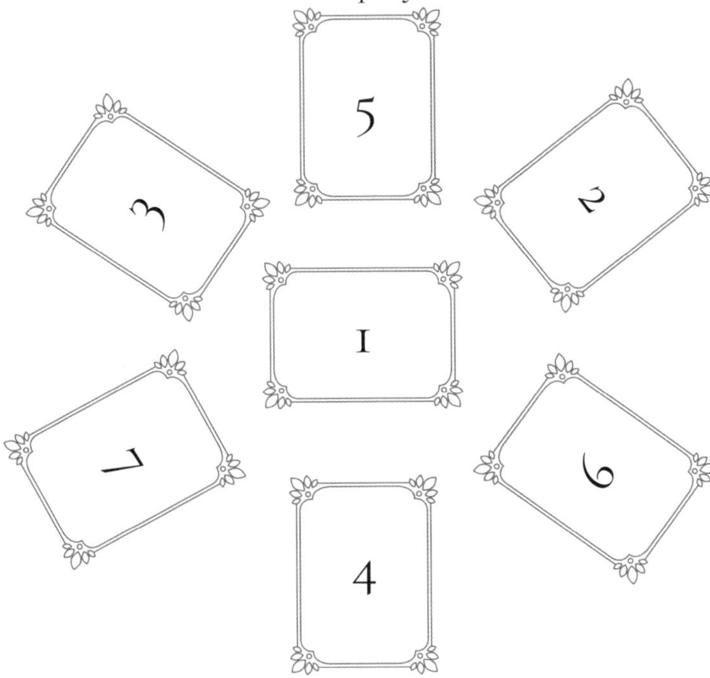

Spread questions

1 - What keeps me tethered and holding on too tight?

2 - How can I release it away to the winds?

3 - What is my warmth on a cold winters night?

Extended spread

4 - How can I harness my own inner light?

5 - What makes me a beacon to others?

6 - Where should I support myself better?

7 - Where can I focus my thoughts at daybreak?

Date: ....../....../......

I am a light and beacon to others with my kindness and healing words.

....

What deck called to me to be used today?

....

What is my own interpretation of each card?

....

....

....

....

....

....

....

....

....

What does my higher self believe the message of the reading to be?

....

....

How does this reading inspire me to take action?

....

....

Numerology and astrology influences

....

Reflective thoughts & feelings	Intuitive messages
....	....
....	....
....	....
....	....
....	....

The Veil

The veil is a spread that asks you to connect with your ancestors and greet them with joy. They will guide you through your reading and into your own light beyond the veil. The spread is laid out in an archway, go gently sweet one.

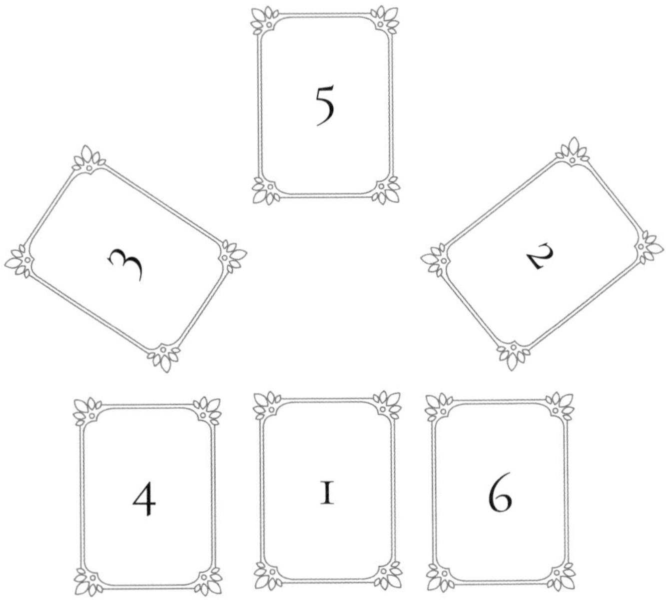

Spread questions

1 - Where am I in this moment in time?

2 - What's in my past that I can't leave behind?

3 - Show me a glimpse of the future tomorrow.

Extended spread

4 - Where can I release angst or sorrow?

5 - What message does my ancestor have for me?

6 - How can I bring them into my life for all to see?

Date: ....../....../......

I embrace the veil and connect with my intuition in my practise.

....

What deck called to me to be used today?

....

What is my own interpretation of each card?

....

....

....

....

....

....

....

....

....

What does my higher self believe the message of the reading to be?

....

....

How does this reading inspire me to take action?

....

....

Numerology and astrology influences

....

Reflective thoughts & feelings

....

....

....

....

....

Intuitive messages

....

....

....

....

....

Evening Enquiry

This spread is a gentle conversation with your higher self to nurture those places you may feel vacant. This spread is laid out as a void in representation of the cosmic force of change.

Spread questions

1 - What disturbs my thoughts?

2 - What drives my reactions?

3 - How can I ease my feelings of lack?

Extended spread

4 - Who supports me when I don't love myself?

5 - What sweet words does my soul long to hear right now?

6 - Send me a message of kindness from my higher self.

Date: ....../....../......

My thoughts do not control me, I am in full control at all times.

....

What deck called to me to be used today?

....

What is my own interpretation of each card?

....

....

....

....

....

....

....

....

....

What does my higher self believe the message of the reading to be?

....

....

How does this reading inspire me to take action?

....

....

Numerology and astrology influences

....

Reflective thoughts & feelings	Intuitive messages
....	....
....	....
....	....
....	....
....	....

I Love Me

A sweet spread for self love and openness to oneself. The spread is laid like a chalice, as in the Star tarot card, to pour love back into yourself.

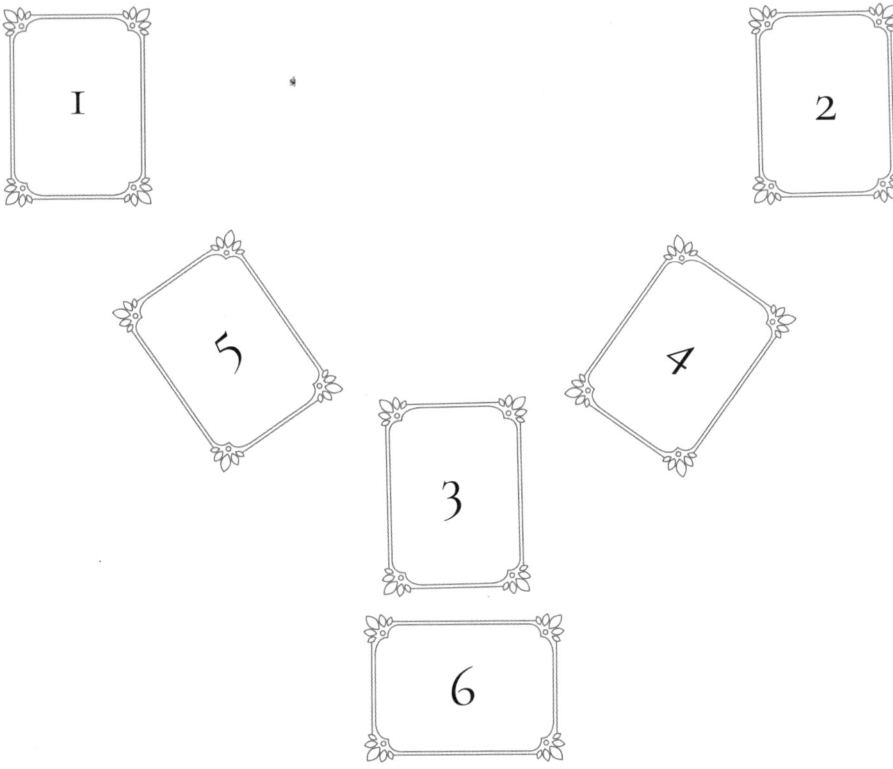

Spread questions

1 - Why don't I value myself more?

2 - How can I be more authentic?

3 - What is my greatest achievement?

Extended spread

4 - What is not worthy of my love?

5 - Where am I drained?

6 - How can I express myself freely?

Date: ....../....../......

I make valuable changes so I can honour my connection to source.

....

What deck called to me to be used today?

....

What is my own interpretation of each card?

....

....

....

....

....

....

....

....

....

What does my higher self believe the message of the reading to be?

....

....

How does this reading inspire me to take action?

....

....

Numerology and astrology influences

....

Reflective thoughts & feelings	Intuitive messages
....	....
....	....
....	....
....	....
....	....

Branches of Me

A spread for expanding open conversation to aid emotional growth. Laid out in the shape of a tree representing new pathways and branches.

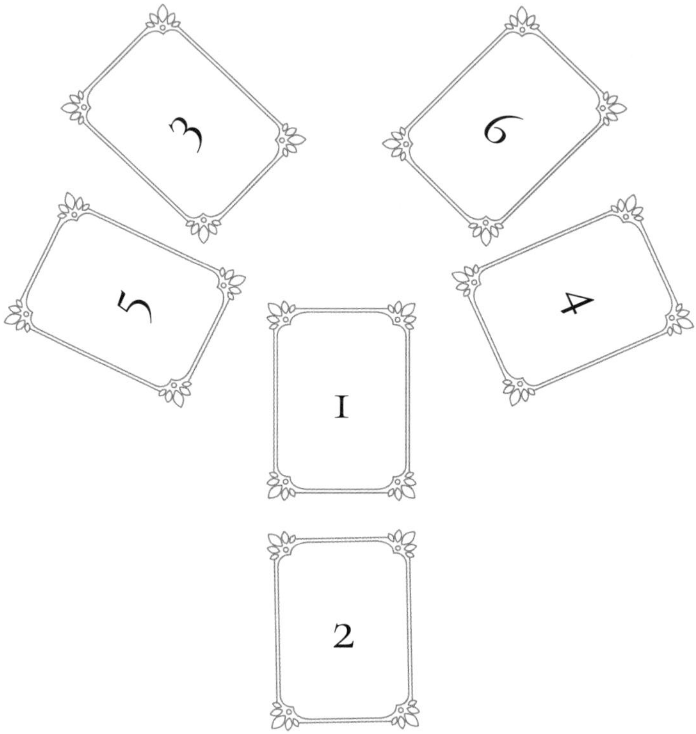

Spread questions

1 - What core of my trunk can I take action to change?
2 - What roots have rotted and need to be removed?
3 - Where can I find space to grow new shoots?

Extended spread

4 - Show me what attributes I should actively share with others?
5 - Where do I hold myself back and hide?
6 - What should I lean towards at this time?

Date: ....../....../......

I change my thought process to help me grow at my greatest rate.

....

What deck called to me to be used today?

....

What is my own interpretation of each card?

....

....

....

....

....

....

....

....

....

What does my higher self believe the message of the reading to be?

....

....

How does this reading inspire me to take action?

....

....

Numerology and astrology influences

....

Reflective thoughts & feelings	Intuitive messages
....	....
....	....
....	....
....	....
....	....

Waning Moon

The waning moon is a time to find inner peace and reconnect with yourself. Of course, it's laid out in a beautiful waning moon too.

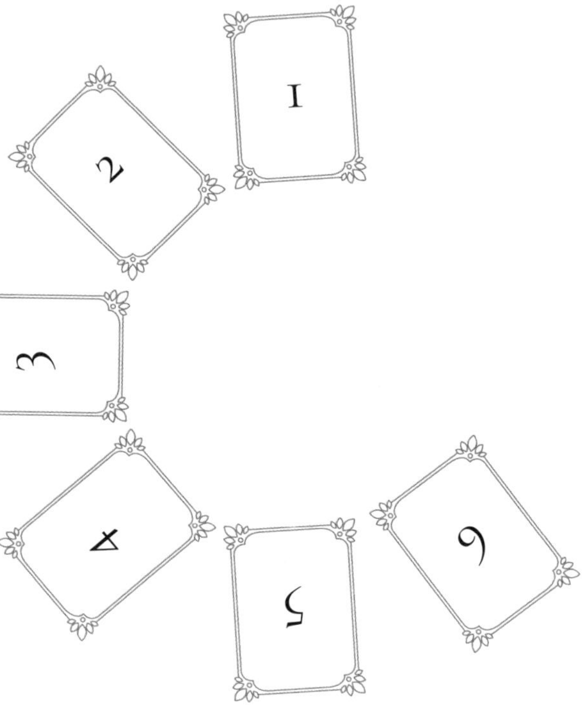

Spread questions

1 - Show me what I must begin to accept?

2 - What holds me back in my shadow self?

3 - What lesson will I learn during this phase?

Extended spread

4 - How am I resisting necessary changes at this time?

5 - Where can I focus my energy on healing and growing?

6 - What ideas must I shed in order to be reborn?

Date: ....../....../......

I find inner peace and reconnect with myself wholly.

What deck called to me to be used today?

What is my own interpretation of each card?

What does my higher self believe the message of the reading to be?

How does this reading inspire me to take action?

Numerology and astrology influences

Reflective thoughts & feelings

Intuitive messages

Meet My Soul

This spread is for those who wish to have a deeper conversation with self. It is laid out in parallels to represent the conscious and the soul.

Spread questions

1 - How does my soul feel right now?

2 - How can I better my connection with my soul?

3 - What does my soul want to show me?

Extended spread

4 - How can I tune into my soul connection with deeper intensity?

5 - What must I release my hold on in order to appease my soul?

6 - A message my soul wants to share with me.

Date: ....../....../......

I am the soul, I am whole, I am connected with my spiritual self.

What deck called to me to be used today?

What is my own interpretation of each card?

What does my higher self believe the message of the reading to be?

How does this reading inspire me to take action?

Numerology and astrology influences

Reflective thoughts & feelings

Intuitive messages

My Purpose

A spread to discover where you can grow your aspirations and the shadows that may hinder you. The upright cards are the soul enquiry, the horizontals are the shadow reflections.

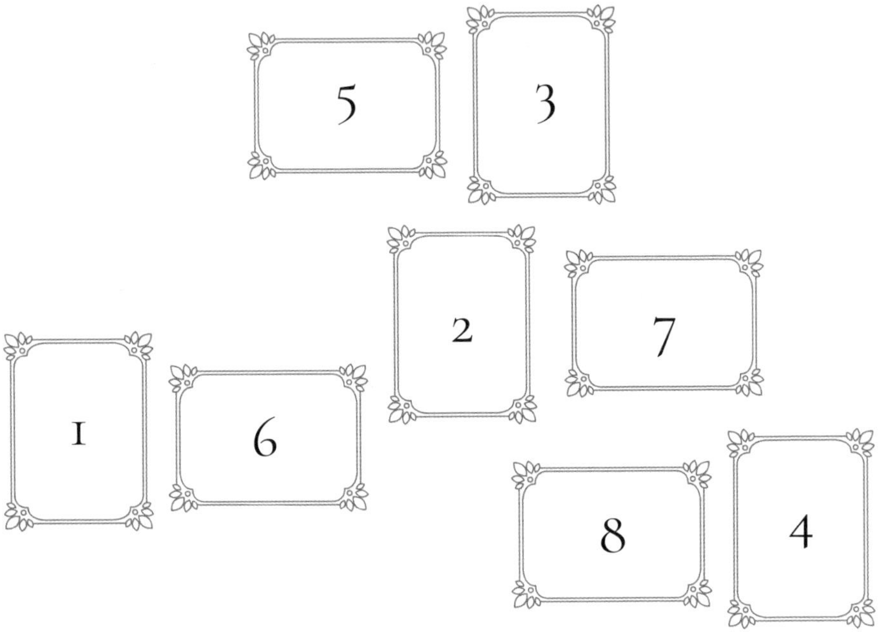

Spread questions

1 - What does my ego-self believe my purpose to be?
2 - What does my soul know my purpose to be?
3 - How can I apply that information to my current situation?
4 - How will this knowledge improve my life?

Extended spread questions

5 - How will it change my current path?
6 - What will hinder my awareness?
7 - Who will challenge this change?
8 - What shadow could block this change?

Date: ....../....../......

My purpose guides me into realms that connect me with my destiny.

....

What deck called to me to be used today?

....

What is my own interpretation of each card?

....

....

....

....

....

....

....

....

....

What does my higher self believe the message of the reading to be?

....

....

How does this reading inspire me to take action?

....

....

Numerology and astrology influences

....

Reflective thoughts & feelings	Intuitive messages
....	....
....	....
....	....
....	....
....	....

Winter Solstice

This spread is to mark a period of reflection on the past year. It mars renewal and the return of the light and is laid out in the shape of a mirror, symbolic of self awareness.

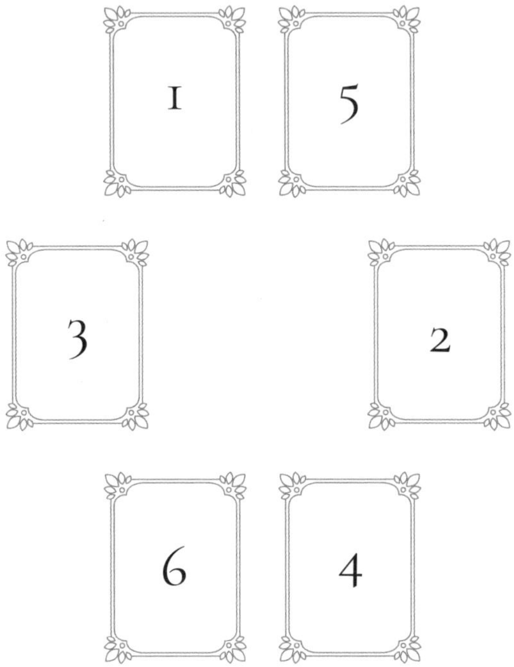

Spread questions

1 - How can I reveal the shadows sitting in my soul right now?
2 - What challenges have they unknowingly presented me?
3 - What is my greatest guiding strength to bring me light?

Extended spread

4 - What lesson has given me the greatest boost?
5 - What seeds of potential are waiting to emerge?
6 - How can I bring in a wonderful rebirth this coming year?

Date: ....../....../......

I am being open and honest with the shadows I need to give light to.

....

What deck called to me to be used today?

....

What is my own interpretation of each card?

....

....

....

....

....

....

....

....

....

What does my higher self believe the message of the reading to be?

....

....

How does this reading inspire me to take action?

....

....

Numerology and astrology influences

....

Reflective thoughts & feelings	Intuitive messages
....	....
....	....
....	....
....	....
....	....

Hygge

This spread is a hug in a mug, a spread of self care. Hygge is a Danish word meaning cosiness and comfort and this spread is about feeling comfortable as you are.

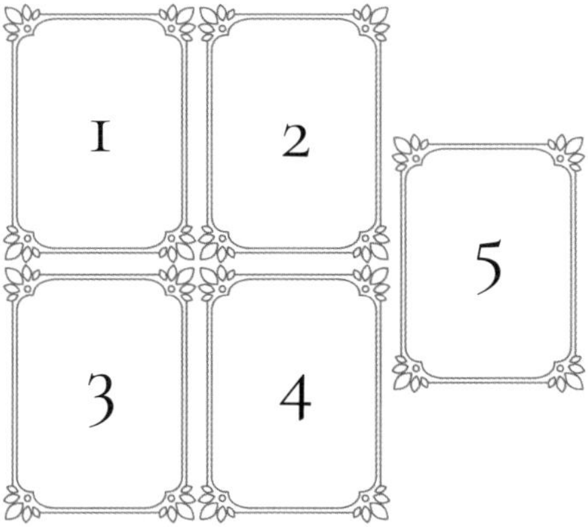

Spread questions

1 - What aspects of my life are in need of rest?
2 - How can I nourish my soul?
3 - What comforts or indulgences should I allow myself?
4 - What inner work should I be focusing on this season?
5 - What light must I shine more brightly with the world?

Date: ....../....../......

I am always the light in my life and I shine my love brightly on others too.

....

What deck called to me to be used today?

....

What is my own interpretation of each card?

....

....

....

....

....

....

....

....

....

What does my higher self believe the message of the reading to be?

....

....

How does this reading inspire me to take action?

....

....

Numerology and astrology influences

....

Reflective thoughts & feelings

....

....

....

....

....

Intuitive messages

....

....

....

....

....

I'm Frozen

This spread is about thawing of our emotions. It is laid out in an icicle symbolic of being transformed after difficulties.

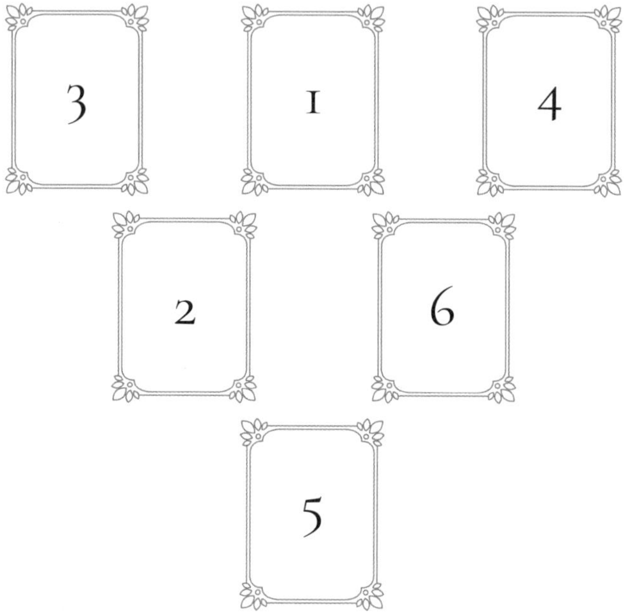

Spread questions

1 - What emotions or feelings have been suppressed?

2 - What steps can I take to thaw these emotions?

3 - What new emotional perspectives will reveal themselves?

Extended spread

4 - How can I tune into these new insights with ease?

5 - What source of comfort will thaw my cold feelings?

6 - Show me the way to release these feelings in love.

Date: ....../....../......

I believe in the power of transformation and I heal my shadows with love.

....

What deck called to me to be used today?

....

What is my own interpretation of each card?

....

....

....

....

....

....

....

....

....

What does my higher self believe the message of the reading to be?

....

....

How does this reading inspire me to take action?

....

....

Numerology and astrology influences

....

Reflective thoughts & feelings	Intuitive messages
....	....
....	....
....	....
....	....
....	....

Yule Blessings

Yuletide is about honouring the shift from one year to another and making plans for the future you. This spread is laid out in the shape of the Yule log to mark the changing of the seasons.

Spread questions

1 - What blessings or gifts do have in my life?
2 - What blessings can I offer to others who need them?
3 - How can I celebrate all the blessings in my life?

Extended spread

4 - What needs to be purged before the next year?
5 - Where can I build new foundations for the next year?
6 - How can I celebrate my achievements this year?

Date: ....../....../......

I am welcoming in healthy new foundations for this new year.

....

What deck called to me to be used today?

....

What is my own interpretation of each card?

....

....

....

....

....

....

....

....

....

What does my higher self believe the message of the reading to be?

....

....

How does this reading inspire me to take action?

....

....

Numerology and astrology influences

....

Reflective thoughts & feelings

....

....

....

....

....

Intuitive messages

....

....

....

....

....

Winter Wisdom

This is a retrospective spread, designed to guide you into a state of peace and assuredness. The spread is laid out in the shape of a key to symbolise the potential of new discoveries and possibilities.

Spread questions

1 - What areas of my life need introspection?
2 - How can I gain wisdom whilst in solitude?
3 - What guidance is available to me from mentors or peers?

Extended spread

4 - What truths am I ready to discover?
5 - What understanding have I gained this year?
6 - How will I integrate this going forward?
7 - Are there any blockages that I need to heal or reveal?
8 - A message from Source for my future.

Date: ....../....../......

I am fearless in the face of new horizons and am exited for my future life.

....

What deck called to me to be used today?

....

What is my own interpretation of each card?

....

....

....

....

....

....

....

....

....

What does my higher self believe the message of the reading to be?

....

....

How does this reading inspire me to take action?

....

....

Numerology and astrology influences

....

Reflective thoughts & feelings	**Intuitive messages**
....	....
....	....
....	....
....	....
....	....

Create Your Own

Date: ....../....../......

Create your own affirmation relating to your spread.

....

What deck called to me to be used today?

....

What is my own interpretation of each card?

....

....

....

....

....

....

....

....

....

What does my higher self believe the message of the reading to be?

....

....

How does this reading inspire me to take action?

....

....

Numerology and astrology influences

....

Reflective thoughts & feelings	Intuitive messages
....	....
....	....
....	....
....	....
....	....

Create Your Own

Date: ....../....../......

Create your own affirmation relating to your spread.

....

What deck called to me to be used today?

....

What is my own interpretation of each card?

....

....

....

....

....

....

....

....

....

What does my higher self believe the message of the reading to be?

....

....

How does this reading inspire me to take action?

....

....

Numerology and astrology influences

....

Reflective thoughts & feelings	Intuitive messages
....	....
....	....
....	....
....	....
....	....